# KENNY BALL'S AND JOHN BENNETT'S MUSICAL SKYLARKS

*A Medley of Memories*

# KENNY BALL'S AND JOHN BENNETT'S MUSICAL SKYLARKS

*A Medley of Memories*

**By Kenny Ball and John Bennett**
**Foreword by Digby Fairweather**

APEX PUBLISHING LTD

# Apex Publishing Ltd

PO Box 7086, Clacton on Sea, Essex, CO15 5WN, England
**www.apexpublishing.co.uk**

**British Library Cataloguing-in-Publication Data**
**A catalogue record for this book**
**is available from the British Library**

ISBN HARDBACK:     1-906358-98-2          978-1-906358-98-3

Typeset in 10pt Baskerville Win95BT
Production Manager: Chris Cowlin
Cover Design: Siobhan Smith

Printed and bound in Great Britain by
MPG Biddles Ltd., King's Lynn, Norfolk

# CONTENTS

ACKNOWLEDGEMENTS                                    vi

FOREWORD BY DIGBY FAIRWEATHER                       vii

1.   IN DAYS OF YORE                                1

2.   EARLY MUSICAL MEMORIES                         11

3.   GOING PRO                                      26

4.   THE KENNY BALL BAND                            38

5.   ON THE ROAD                                    50

6.   THE HIT YEARS                                  63

7.   THE TV YEARS                                   90

8.   BEHIND THE IRON CURTAIN                        106

9.   ROUND THE WORLD                                133

10.   HERE AND THERE                                160

11.   MY GUYS                                       182

12.   TALKING ABOUT ME                              197

EPILOGUE                                            203

# ACKNOWLEDGEMENTS

Kenny and I would like to express our gratitude to two special people for their sterling efforts over many years in keeping the day-to-day running of this band on track. Firstly, for her steadfast support, her always bright and friendly approach – and last but certainly not least, for suggesting Apex Publishing Ltd as our publisher! – the Gold award goes to Kenny's personal secretary, Heather Lewis.

Our thanks also to Phil Hoy, custodian of the Kenny Ball Appreciation Society and editor of its magazine *The Jazzette*, whose detailed knowledge of the band's history is second to none.

*Heather can be contacted by e-mail at heather@raylewis.co.uk*

*Phil's phone number is 0113 2637075*

# FOREWORD
## By Digby Fairweather

Have you ever noticed how some of the words in our beautiful English language get devalued? For me, that's the case here, because when I say that writing a foreword to this definitive book about Kenny Ball is an honour, it somehow doesn't sound like much. So let's go to the dictionary for a proper definition. An 'honour' is - according to the *Oxford English Dictionary* - both 'a privilege and/or pleasure' and/or 'an outward admission of great respect and esteem'.

All those terms apply here, because Kenny - for hundreds of thousands of fans worldwide - represents something virtually unique in the up-hill-and-down-dale landscape of jazz in Britain. For me, to begin with - amongst many in the British trumpet fraternity - he represents both a role model and an idol. A baby boomer, born in 1946, I was hopelessly in love with both jazz and the trumpet by the age of ten. In my mid-teens I was vividly aware of a newly announced presence on the scene from the brassy exuberance of his introduction to 'Samantha' - a hit-parade reworking of Cole Porter's tune from *High Society*, which stayed in the charts for 15 weeks from February 1961. There were plenty of trumpeters around at that time whose talents stood out; notably (in the Dixieland music I secretly preferred) Freddy Randall and Humphrey Lyttelton, Colin Smith and Pat Halcox. But here, plainly, was a player who set challenging new standards for every instrumental contemporary in Britain's jazz scene. For the next two or three years I both watched and heard my new hero effortlessly maintaining his position in the public eye and ear, and for the next 50 more I have continued to watch him steadily consolidating it as that rarest of beings: a British jazzman who has won for himself what every fellow contender wishes for on a star - a household name.

"Like Harpic," Kenny would respond in what (to be fair) is a well-rehearsed one liner, "-clean round the bend!" But that very response is another reason why writing about him is for me both a pleasure and that honour I mentioned, because - for a trumpeter who over the years has conquered the international jazz scene and endeared himself to hundreds of thousands of general listeners that otherwise seem to think they don't like jazz - Kenny Ball possesses none of the ego or self-glorification that are all too often apparent in the less-talented rock 'n' roll fraternity that followed him into the public eye as the 1960s moved on. To conquer that comprehensive pop invasion (which to all intents and purposes closed down the high-profile jazz scene for all but two of Kenny's contemporaries) required a remarkable talent, a spectacular track record in the hit parade and an ability, like any master-mariner, to forge ahead above the fickle - and regularly ruthless - tides of popular fashion. Yet, despite such a challenge, Kenny has maintained that most elusive of qualities in this sometimes ill-mannered twenty-first century: the bearing and values of - another devalued word - a *gentleman*, which - back to our dictionary again - is properly defined as 'a man possessing innate qualities of human refinement including courtesy, judgement, generosity and fortitude'. I learned about at least one of these qualities quite early on in my own jazz life. After a packed Sunday afternoon concert by Kenny Ball's Jazzmen at the end of Southend's 'longest pier in the world' I rode back on the pier train and spied my hero making for his car. As he closed the door, I knocked on the window and saw it obligingly rolled down.

"Please, Mr Ball," I asked, "Could you tell me the trumpet

fingering for top A, B and C?"

Kenny paused and cocked his head. "Yes," he said, "valves one and two, then middle, then open! Is that okay?" And with a smile and a wave he sped away.

A generous spirit, then as now. And almost 50 years on - despite his modest assertions to the contrary - I simply don't know anyone that doesn't like Kenny Ball for exactly such reasons.

Of course, in artistic terms alone, that's (unfortunately) of no consequence. But, returning to his musical talents for now, there was no doubt, from the first years of his career, that Kenny's trumpet playing was truly outstanding and also that his terms of influence were much broader than most of his fellow players on the Revivalist jazz scene. Back in the late 1940s he was just as able to absorb the bebop revolutions of Dizzy Gillespie as to revere the founding musical tenets of Louis Armstrong (as well - even before Louis - as another hero, the great Bunny Berigan). And I have another small personal memory of winning a competition (set, around 1962, by *Melody Maker*, Britain's longest-running music weekly) to name his favourite trumpeters. which -remarkably for a player known for his abiding affection for Traditional jazz - I knew to be Armstrong, Bix Beiderbecke and Clifford Brown. His respect for Brown (the man that Miles Davis called "the best bebop trumpeter"), as well as hours of daily practice, equipped Kenny Ball to deal with the tight discipline of Sid Phillips' tightly arranged Dixieland ensembles just as easily as to work with Eric Delaney's poll-winning big band, in which he could - and did - race joyfully through an express-speed trumpet feature on Ray Noble's 'Cherokee', a tune that (particularly in its middle section!) has harmonically challenged jazz musicians of every stylistic persuasion from that day to this. And when, in consequence, all of this mental energy and technical equipment was finally let loose at the head of his chosen band from 1958, it's no wonder that Kenny Ball and his Jazzmen speedily overtook most their contemporaries for technical polish, fire and swaggering creativity, whether in arrangement or solo flight. Notably, it was critic Steve Race - a premier commentator of the period in print and on radio as well as a highly skilled pianist that knew exactly what was good and what wasn't - who first publicly declared his undying allegiance to the young trumpeter and his band; a group much more recently described by critic Brian Morton (in *The Penguin Guide to Jazz on CD*) as "a tough, hard-hitting outfit which its powerful leader directed with great skill".

With due respect to good friend Brian, his description could hardly be expected to match the thrill of watching Kenny Ball's Jazzmen in action back then. Dressed in electric-grey tailor-made suits, they would race through a concert programme matched for its imagination (everything from Jelly Roll Morton's 'Grandpa's Spells' to Humphrey Lyttelton's 'Baby Doll') by the blazing, unconquerable trumpet of the leader. But he was by no means carrying a troupe of lesser sidemen. Trombonist John Bennett (of whom much more later), as well as clarinettist Dave Jones and pianist Ron Weatherburn, matched up to their leader with equivalent inspiration and technical panache. Suffice it to say that all the cornermen of Kenny Ball's Jazzmen were international-standard musicians who produced the first serious threat to America since the USA finally turned the tables on the British in 1783. And during their first tour in 1962, when the Ball band mounted a triumphant musical sortie on Art Hodes' club in Chicago, their victory was duly recalled to me years later by American guitarist Marty Grosz. "We couldn't believe it," said Marty. "We'd never heard of Kenny Ball until all of a sudden this British band were top of the American charts with some tune called 'Midnight in Moscow'. Even Eddie

Condon covered it, which was unthinkable! And when they got to the club they quite simply played us out of the room and down the street!"

Talking of the charts brings to mind that anyone under the age of - well, let's say 40! - may indeed not remember that, back before the rock set in around 1963, Kenny Ball (and his Jazzmen) were authentic pop stars as well as premier league jazz musicians. As his current entry in the online encyclopedia 'Wikipedia' reminds us: in July 1962 he appeared on the front cover of *New Musical Express* (*Melody Maker*'s chief rival) in the company of (Sir) Cliff Richard, Joe Brown, Brenda Lee, Frank Ifield and his co-star in the hit film *It's Trad, Dad!*, Craig Douglas. But such a situation - extraordinary though it may seem today - is easily explained for those with an eye to popular music history. Good-looking Kenny Ball (who could in those days have easily passed for Errol Flynn) and his equally charismatic young band (a contemporary picture of his group bears the legend: '"all my boys are so handsome," says Kenny Ball!') had emerged at the exact point at which the once-ethnic Traditional jazz movement of the 1950s was about to ignite into mass popularity - a boom that would only be itself blown away by (as we've said) the arrival of The Beatles, The Rolling Stones and the comprehensive cultural revolution of rock music that followed on. In the meantime, Kenny Ball and his Jazzmen looked good and sounded wonderful.

When rock 'n' roll and The Beatles finally cemented the transformation of popular music trends forever, I know for a fact that - however remarkably - neither Kenny nor his Jazzmen were greatly affected. Instead, as the years went by they turned into beloved pillars of Britain's popular music establishment on both television and radio and also in concert halls. Admittedly, within a year or so from 1963, jazz clubs (the national 'milk round' of small venues that had birthed the Trad Boom) had gone for good, given over universally to the new and engulfing waves of rock and R&B. But the legacy of hit records by his band (14 in all, beginning with 'Samantha' in February in 1961 and finally concluding with an amiable cover of The Beatles' 'When I'm 64' in July 1967) ensured that, for as long as he wanted to continue, Kenny Ball's career would be safe. And, as you'll read in the pages that follow, that continues to be the case in 2010.

What I suspect was far more threatening to this young bandleader was the unexpected onset (as the Trad Boom finally foundered around 1964) of what all trumpet players fear: a condition most commonly called 'lip trouble'. More specifically, this entails inadvertent strain or misuse of the tiny yet immensely complex corporation of muscles around the mouth (technically called the 'embouchure') against which the player sets his mouthpiece. 'Lip trouble' hangs over all trumpeters like an ever-present evil spirit, is worryingly easy to acquire (particularly under the pressure of continual playing) and can take years in the correction. And, as a fellow sufferer (for over a decade from 1987), I know very well that the feeling of a gift suddenly and rudely denied is equivalent to musical castration. The fact that Kenny Ball acquired the problem in the mid-1960s (when he was somewhere very close to the peak of his high-profile career) and then dealt with it on both a mental and physical level, thereafter returning to form with extraordinary speed, says a huge amount for the inward strength, artistic tenacity and admirable personal fortitude of this quite remarkable man. When he and his Jazzmen shared four concerts in London with Louis Armstrong's All Stars (I saw them all) in 1968 it was as if nothing had ever been wrong. At that point Louis called Kenny "a genius". And while no jazz trumpeter has ever been able to match the consummate artistry of Armstrong, it would also be true to say that Kenny Ball had nothing to fear from the presence on the same stage of the man that Wynton Marsalis christened "The Shakespeare of Jazz".

It was for such reasons of respect and admiration, as well as privileged friendship, that, when four years after its publication Kenny expressed dissatisfaction with his (ghost-written) autobiography called *Blowing My Own Trumpet* in 2009, I offered to help him write a new one. We'd only got a short way into the project before musical commitments made my visits to his (then) home in Stansted less regular than they should have been. Consequently, aware that I was letting a respected friend down very badly, I asked Kenny's trombonist John Bennett if he might help me out, and John kindly agreed. It had already occurred to me that, as Kenny Ball's musical partner of over 50 years (they co-formed the Jazzmen in 1958), John would be the ideal collaborator with his leader; and, as the band's librarian, his beautifully assembled scrapbooks would provide the perfect, accurate source material both to pin down memories and to prompt new ones.

My only mild surprise was when ever-modest John, whose natural charm matches his superb musicianship, asked me to explain in this Foreword who he was and why he should be considered co-author. "Kenny's a household name," he said, "and he's been around for more than half a century. All right, I may have been around just as long, but I'm just a backroom boy really - merely a name in my *own* household. I can claim to have been in Kenny's band for as long as Kenny himself, and even before Kenny founded his Jazzmen we both worked together in another band. But in all that time I've always been what in this business we call a sideman - someone who contributes without making too much of a fuss about it."

Anyone that has followed the Traditional area of British jazz will appreciate the level of John's understatement here. At the time when his leader's band was formed in 1958, trombonists that played Dixieland music in Britain were a mixed bunch; players that embraced a variety of styles ranging from hopeful aspirations towards the sophistication of a Jack Teagarden to the demolition-squad attack of a Trummy Young, the tailgate style of Kid Ory and - right down at the amateur end of the craft - the roars and rasps that reminded the great American trombonist Vic Dickenson of "a dying cow in a thunderstorm". When John arrived on the scene in the later 1950s he combined a built-in technical superiority with the kind of driving solo creativity required to match his leader's challenging new standards, and he was quickly singled out by premier critics like Steve Race as a supremely gifted new arrival. Given John's eternally positive approach to life, undiminished talents and handsome, youthful demeanour, this seems to suggest, uncannily, that over 50 years later nothing has changed.

Beyond his musical gifts, though, John has other talents supremely fitted for his co-author's role in this new book. "I'm now regarded as the band archivist," he explained with the characteristic modesty of self-expression that has endeared him to friends and colleagues the world over, "which means that I squirrel away any kind of tat relating to the band which most people would chuck straight in the bin. Ask my wife". The 'tat', you may not be surprised to hear, comprises - amongst much else - a trio of exquisitely maintained computer-based scrapbooks, which would in themselves keep any British jazz fan (as they kept me when this book was first mooted) happy for hours. But while the scrapbooks would have made a fine independent chronicle in their own right, there were other reasons for the creation of this book.

"The idea really dates back several years to one long, boozy session of reminiscing between Kenny and me," John explained to me in January 2011. "We're both getting on a bit - Kenny at 80 is getting on a bit ahead of me, in fact – and, like old codgers the world over, we do like to recall past times. But that evening over a glass or two, we had a marathon sitting; we must have dredged up memories to fill a dozen books. The trouble was that the following day neither of us could remember a word of what had passed between us!

"So we decided that one day we would make the effort to write a book. In the years since then the idea was put aside and forgotten. But now that the opportunity has arisen for a new book about Kenny and the band I thought it might be a good idea to return to that original theme - our night of boozy reminiscences. So we armed ourselves with a couple of mini sound recorders and over the ensuing weeks just went to town with whatever memories sprang to mind - each of us having fun sparking the other on. [As the author of a couple of jazz biographies and long-time interviewer, I know that this is absolutely the best - and possibly the only - way to keep the stories coming!]

"I have also contributed some personal extracts from diaries I kept between the early sixties up to the nineties. And both Ken and I have included reminiscences that extend back to our childhood - long before our paths first crossed. We've ended up with a dialogue that starts off some distance apart, then comes together - a kind of duet."

And a grand musical saga it is, too. Writing your Foreword, Kenny and John - as I said three thousand words ago - is an honour and a privilege. And, of course - just like they say in the song - thank you for the music, too.

*With respect and affection,*

**Digby Fairweather**
*9 January 2011*

www.apexpublishing.co.uk

# 1
# IN DAYS OF YORE

***Kenny:***

I was born in 1930, the last of seven children, to Ethel and James Ball in Mayesbrook Road, part of the Dagenham Council Estate, which had only just been built. Officially it was part of Ilford - so 'officially' I was born in Ilford. One of my brothers died when I was four years old, and I remember him being taken out of the house in a wooden box. He'd died of TB and I wasn't allowed to go in the room due to the risk of catching it.

Soon afterwards the family moved down to Worcester, where I started my schooling. My dad got a job with bookbinders Ebenezer Bayliss. Dad was a master bookbinder and helped to develop the paperback book. I took up the violin for a little while in 1938, but one day it got smashed on the way home from school - because only 'sissies' played violin back then! So I took up the mouth organ instead. Pretty soon I moved on to the chromatic harmonica - Mum and Dad bought me one for Christmas - because I couldn't find all the notes I wanted to play on the ordinary harmonica. Although it was difficult to start with, I finally mastered it and actually became fairly professional at it, too, I think, and I really got to like it. Larry Adler was the king of the harmonica back then, and there was also a group around called The Harmonicats. They had mouth organs of all sizes - some about a yard long and some so small that you could stick them up your nose, I reckon. Mine was of a regular size and I could play about an octave and a half on it.

I think I was very fortunate to have a terrific ear for music. I

1

could hear a tune and more or less play it on the harmonica straightaway, which was great when it came to trying to play jazz later on. And I still play it now.

I gave my daughter a blues harmonica of mine on her 55th birthday and made a joke out of it, telling her, "This is a present from the Essex Harmonica Appreciation Society, and you've won first prize." She'd love to play the harmonica, but she can't. She's as funny as hell. We were in Puerto Banús on the Costa del Sol a while ago, and one evening we went to a place where bands play.

My daughter's husband and my son, Keith, went up to the bandleader and said, "Do you know you've got one of the top female blues harmonica players in here tonight?"

He replied, "Really? Would she like to come up for a blow?"

"Yes, we'll try to persuade her."

So they called her up to play and my daughter started panicking, shrieking, "I can't play, I can't play!"

"I'll tell you what," I said to her, "I'll start and you come in later and fill in."

So there I was, blowing away, and when I finally stopped and gave her the nod she blew into the thing and it just sort of went "Fwweeerrrrr!!"

And the place erupted! She got a standing ovation for that! In response, she acted the part. They're good kids, wonderful children, and I love 'em - I love all children!

My parents both liked music and Dad, who was born in 1888, was a piccolo player in the Territorial Army before the First World War. Mum was born in 1887 and they were living in the East End back then. Both my dad and my mum had run away from home and they met in the East End of London. By all accounts, my dad was a bit of a lad! At one point he'd had his arm burnt by my granny - she took the poker out of the fire and burnt his arm. And he still had the scar, I remember. But he was good to me. I had the best upbringing that any child could possibly want. My life as a child was full of sunshine, music, everything a kid could ask for.

There was always music in the house. Mum didn't play, but my sister Ethel played a bit of piano, sister Marge sang soprano, and my brother Ted got a tea-chest bass. Every Sunday Dad used to get on his piccolo and jaw harp and they used to play songs like 'I'll Be Loving You Always'. I always remember that one. Of course, the piano was never tuned - we couldn't afford it - so you can imagine the terrible noises coming out! That was our Sunday afternoon, just about as far back as I can remember.

My mother really was a marvellous lady. One of my earliest memories of her is back in Seven Kings, kneeling on the floor, washing the lino. I remember waving my finger at her and saying, "Mum, you get up! I never want to see you doing that again." So the first thing I bought her when I earned some money was a washing machine, followed by a refrigerator. She used to light the fire on a Monday morning to boil the water for washing in a big stone tub. That makes her sound like a real working-class lady - if there is such a thing these days - but that wasn't really the case. Her sister, our Auntie Alice, was a district nurse and I think nurses were considered the 'upper echelon' of the working class, for want of a better phrase. So it wasn't really a working-class background. In fact, my mother's family came from a theatrical background. Her father was supposed to be the stage manager at a big London theatre - either the Gaiety or the Adelphi, I'm not sure which - though in reality he was probably only the carpenter or something! My brother Jim said he owned a silver button belonging to one of our ancestors who was a captain at the Battle of Trafalgar. Our Auntie Alice used to say he abused my mum and that's why she moved out to the East End. I've got some of my mum's nature, basically. She was very kind. When anyone came to the house - however corny this sounds - the front door was always open. And if anybody needed a meal, or a slice of bread, butter and jam, or a cup of tea, they could have it right away.

### John:

*I was born in 1936, within the sound of Bow Bells, which makes me a true Cockney I suppose - if you can believe my dad. He used to say he'd heard a ringing in his ears the moment I popped out, which he reckoned was Bow Bells calling. As he was so determined that any son of his would have to be a regular little Cockney chip-off-the-old-block, I've always taken his word for it.*

*I was christened shortly before the accession of King Edward VIII, which at the time was thought to be a good omen. So, in celebration of the dawning of this glorious new age, I was given the middle name Edward.*

*Within weeks the 'omen' turned out to be a dud. Edward VIII had been dating an American divorcee, which posed all kinds of constitutional problems. And I was going through some constitutional problems of my own - I had pneumonia. Things went from bad to worse for the King and I: at about the same time as the Royal Crisis hit the national press, I hit a crisis, too. My mother, who had been nursing me at the hearth in front of a coal fire, noticed that my lips had turned blue and I'd stopped breathing. Before she could call for help, an avalanche of soot plummeted down the chimney and clouded into our parlour. Within seconds the room received a change of decor, from a dingy beige to an even dingier matt black.*

*Owing to the general confusion, no one in the family remembers what happened next. But according to Cockney folklore, soot is lucky stuff; so getting half a ton of it dumped on us might've been just what the doctor ordered! In any event, the Last of the Cockney Bennetts survived his crisis - which is more than can be said for his royal namesake. Shortly afterwards the King chucked in his hand and abdicated. During the short reign of Edward VIII the Crystal Palace had been destroyed by fire, civil war had flared up in Spain, and Hitler was scheming to conquer the world. So much for the New Age.*

### Kenny:

The war came along, and we moved back to London and lived in Seven Kings, or Goodmayes as it was then - just in time for the start of the Blitz! We had a house backing onto the railway yards and, of course, the Germans with their Focke-wulfs, Messerschmitts, Dorniers, or whatever, would come straight up the railway line from Southend, see our backyard with all the goods trains in it and drop their load there. In my mind I can see them now. But you don't get scared as little kids. That goes for the older ones, too, come to that. You don't see the old men - the people that make the war in the first place - actually going to war. They get the 17- or 18-year-old kids who sometimes think they're fireproof. 'Nothing can happen to me, I'll sort them out!' - that sort of attitude. But when you get into your mid-20s it's a bit of a different matter. My dad was 26 when he went to the trenches in the First World War, but all his mates were 17 and 18, so I think he must have put a protective coat on. "Over the top, Cecil! No, after you, Claude …!"

My brothers all joined up. One brother was in the Navy - at least I called him my brother, but actually he was a cousin. My mother adopted two children, but later on we worked out that she brought up 25 children in all. My dad, you see, had a couple of brothers and they both fought in the First World War like him. One was killed and the other was shell-shocked during his time in the Artillery, so he went a bit doolally. My mum took over the care of his children. There were others, like my Uncle Bill and Auntie Alice, who were always round the house. As one started work and finally left home, another youngster would come in. I was very fond of my dad - a marvellous man. He was terribly down to earth and could never say no. And when I say

5

that, I mean he would never give up on anything. I inherited that quality from my father.

I won't say I was demanding, but yes, I suppose I was spoilt because I was the youngest of seven children and, with two more adopted, that made it nine. I was the last of the nine. Unfortunately, all of them are dead now. The last one, brother Jimmy, died two years ago. He was about 95, I suppose. He was in the Fire Brigade during the Blitz; saw some terrible things, apparently. He lived in the same house all the way through his adult life. He got married around 1934, and when he died in 2007 he was taken out of the very same council house. A mean man really, I suppose. He really was. When my dad had to give up his allotment in the late 1980s Jim went around my dad's house, picked up all his tools and said, "Dad, you won't need these anymore." I went off brother Jim then. I've seen a lot of that sort of thing: like daughters going around to visit their mums on their deathbeds and saying, "You've got a nice hat there, and you won't need that anymore, will you?" Incredible.

I was particularly close to my brother Ted, a very brave man. He was in the war - joined the RAF as an engineer, then learned to fly. He did 75 operational missions in a Halifax bomber - about three times as many as anyone's supposed to survive. You were lucky if you came back after one mission. First of all he did 13 or 14 raids over the Ruhr in Germany, and then over North Africa - Algeria. He also dropped spies and weapons into Yugoslavia, Italy and the south of France. He was awarded the Croix de Guerre for shoving Frenchmen with parachutes out of planes. Some of them didn't want to go, you see. He told me he had to kick them up the backside to get them out of the Halifax, because when the old green light went on you had to go. Flying at three miles a minute, if you didn't go when you were given the signal from down below, you were lost. Lots didn't want to go; in fact some didn't go. They wanted to go home instead!

Ted was the next youngest brother to me. I was the youngest, as I said, and he was eight years older. He'd make bikes for me. He'd go down the dump, get the bits, and make me up a whole bike from what he'd found. And I remember when I was about nine years old he made himself a motorcycle out of spare parts and we used to go down the factory with his motorbike and just drive around, because there was no law then to say a kid can't drive on private land.

They were all in the war, my brothers: Jim was a fireman; Ted was in the Air Force flying Halifaxes, as I said; George was an instrument maker in India and a very clever lad; and Frank was in the Navy on submarines - God knows how he survived it, and in the end he was invalided out. He'd been on deck firing a gun, putting shells in the breach. Then the Germans fired back. He turned around after the impact and saw his mate's head had been blown clean off. I think the shock of that was so great it affected him mentally and the powers-that-be said, "He's had enough of this war." And that was that. I wanted to go to war but I couldn't just then - too young, you see - so I did some riding on a bike for the Fire Service when the telephones were down and helped the wardens out, taking round flasks of tea.

I had quite a good war, but I lost a couple of mates down the road. I was in bed upstairs along with one of the children my mum used to take care of: my nephew Terry, who was 18 months younger than me. We were both in the front upstairs bedroom, lying in bed, at 7 o'clock on the Friday morning, when most of the rest of the house was blown away. That's one way of getting attention: no front to the house! I looked at him and said, "Let's get downstairs quick." No one in our family was killed, but later on a V2 landed on a shelter about 200 yards away, and two of my schoolmates and their family were down there. They just disappeared down a 30ft hole. I can see it now: about five or six houses completely gone and a big hole where that air-raid shelter was ....

## John:

*By the time the War started, our family had moved out of the East End to Potters Bar, north of London, which was almost like being evacuated into the country, so I was never in the thick of the Blitz like Ken. But as our flat was situated on high ground and its front windows looked south, we had a grandstand view of the bombing raids over London from 1940 to '41. I have to say I enjoyed every moment. I was only four.*

*On Blitz nights my grandmother would switch out the lights and draw open our blackout curtains. The noise of anti-aircraft gunfire would wake me up, and in excitement I'd leap out of bed and join her at the window, where together, and in silence, we'd watch the swivelling searchlight beams and see the fire-glow over London gradually spread outwards and upwards during the night into a blood-red semicircle on the southern horizon.*

*Our Morrison indoor shelter arrived on a Council lorry one morning in 1941: a monster Meccano set of angle-irons, wire netting, and a heavy sheet-steel surface that had to be carted by six men. The components were unloaded to steelyard clatterings and muffled swearing and deposited in our front garden. Simultaneous deliveries were made to our neighbours in adjoining ground-floor maisonettes, so that by mid-afternoon it looked as though our street had sent away for a kit to build a battleship.*

*Our new shelter was bolted together in our front room by one of the 'Old Men from the Council'; a wheezy gentleman, far too elderly for call-up and driven almost to death's door by the exhausting task of putting together a Morrison single-handed.*

*When it was finally set up there were too many nuts and bolts left over for my mum's liking: she was worried that some important bits might've been left out. I don't know whether there ever were any cases reported of Morrison shelters collapsing of their own accord and crushing their occupants to strawberry jam, but that danger seemed real enough to my*

8

*mum. She complained to the council man that his Morrison looked rickety, and that she and her family would feel much safer sheltering under our three-foot square dining room table.*

*"Rubbish!" snorted the council man. "You'd have your heads down and your arses up in the air like ostriches."*

*"But our table's made of oak!" protested Mum with female logic.*

*"All right, all right, put it this way," sighed the voice of authority. "Morrison shelters are designed to save lives. If Old Adolf decides to lob one of his bleedin' land-mines on these jerry-built maisonettes, your Morrison may well be the only thing left standing in this road! Think about it," he said.*

*We did. The dining table was dismantled for the duration, and from then until the war's end we ate all our meals off the top of the Morrison and slept under it at night. You could do other things on its steel surface, too: like play table tennis, or jump up and down and make noises like thunder!*

### Kenny:

I went to school in Mayfield Central until I was 14. The school's still there, by the way, though it's been sold now. I missed getting to the South East Technical College; one other bloke called Mason beat me to the remaining space, otherwise I would've stayed on until 16. But I loved school; absolutely loved it. I was Miss Pocock's favourite. What a lovely name for a teacher - Miss Pocock! No oil painting was she, though - she had buck teeth. But she was such a sweet person. I got six of the best a few times from Mr Steer, the Headmaster (caned on the hand) and then Mr Ivy. But I did well at school; I was cricket captain, house captain and athletics captain. And I was top of the class at various other subjects, especially science.

I love science, and I came to love history later on, too. I wasn't terribly keen on it at the time, but I've since developed a penchant for it. I like history books - either fiction or nonfiction; war history in particular - very much so; blood and thunder in general, really. I think that might have a lot to do with my family, too, because as you've seen the Army, Navy and Air Force were a big part of our existence. They were all at war, as I've said - one in a submarine, one in a Halifax bomber and another out in India. Then there was my dad fire-watching and Jim in the fire service, going out every night putting out fires and pulling out burnt bodies. And I remember praying (I've never told this to anybody) and saying, "If you take me, God, I don't mind going to war. But would you please bring all my brothers home." Kind of a weird thing for a kid to say, I suppose. But, as I've said, we were a very close family and I really do miss them all a lot. In fact, I daren't think about them too much, otherwise I get tears in my eyes.

Mind you, my own family make up for it; they're very, very similar. They phone me every day, every one of them. I just had Keith, my son, on the phone. I thought it might've been either Jane, Sophie, Nicole or Gillian. Every one of them phones me at least once a day.

# 2
# EARLY MUSICAL MEMORIES

*Kenny:*

The first record I ever heard that struck me was 'Begin the Beguine' by Artie Shaw. That was in 1940 when I was 10 years old. My brother George bought the record and used to play it all the time. It's a very good tune, especially with that marvellous emotional ending after the musical build-up. That was the first tune. Then, of course, during the war there were all those happy songs: 'We're Going to Hang Out the Washing on the Siegfried Line' and 'Coming In on a Wing and a Prayer'. I remember thinking about my brother Ted when I heard that second one, because he was doing just that in his Halifax bomber. He used to bring home some American airmen when he came home on leave, too - all of them chewing gum galore. But back then you couldn't get anything in the way of American jazz records. Records by the Quintette du Hot Club de France (Hot Club of France Quintet) were the only ones we could get in the war. We didn't get American records and we didn't have the facility to get V-disc records as the American troops did. You only had the ones that were then available commercially, all made in England before the war.

The very first Quintette records I got hold of were 'Between the Devil and the Deep Blue Sea' (with Dickie Wells on trombone, a beautiful player) and 'I Got Rhythm', both featuring classical guitarist Django Reinhardt and trumpeters Bill Coleman, Shad Collins and Bill Dillard from Teddy Hill's band. Shad would've been 15 years older than me then. He came over to England years later with the show One Mo' Time, but I didn't get to meet him.

So I had two records in all - and they both went grey, worn out through constant playing. Oh, and I also got hold of a Bunny Berigan record, the 12-inch one of 'I Can't Get Started' and 'Prisoner's Song', and that was it. Then after the war the English jazz records started coming out: Humphrey Lyttelton with George Webb on the blue Parlophone label's 'Super Rhythm Style' series. I've still got about three of those - '1919 March' was one, and that knocked me out; very traditional jazz. But I was also into bebop at the same time!

I left Mayfield Central School in 1944 and went to work at J. Walter Thompson, the advertising agency. I was 14, and by then I'd started to hear jazz on the radio.

### John:

*In about 1943 one of my uncles gave me a pile of 78s - mostly big band music. We had a wind-up gramophone, and I got quite excited when I heard the first of those records. It was 'Boogie Woogie' by Tommy Dorsey. The thing that caught my imagination was not the glorious big band sound, nor Dorsey's immaculate trombone playing - it was those rhythmic piano bass figures that gave the number its title; even though on this record the piano was barely audible above a background hiss that sounded like someone sandpapering woodwork.*

*As if by magic, not long afterwards a piano arrived at our family home. It belonged to an aunt of mine who'd been bombed out of her home in the East End and needed somewhere to store what furniture she had left. This should've been a heaven-sent opportunity to a budding boogie-woogie freak, so it's a mystery why throughout the war years I never got to grips with that bombed-out piano. Instead, the battle-scarred old upright, its once smoothly polished mahogany surface now abrasive to the touch due to the minute fragments of window glass still imbedded in it, waited silently in our front room for something to happen. Eventually it did; but I now look back on the intervening period as my musical 'gap years'.*

**Kenny:**

In 1945 I started work at Francis, Day and Hunter in Charing Cross Road, selling pianos. But the main thing wasn't really the pianos. There was a record department upstairs, which was right up my alley. I started hearing things like 'Blue Skies' by Duke Ellington, on blue label Parlophone, which had the highest note I'd ever heard on a trumpet. I nearly gave up there and then. Then there was 'Things to Come' by Dizzy Gillespie's big band and all the bebop songs. And, of course, I started to get hold of published music, too. I've still got some of it actually; the old tunes, and some of what they called 'transcripts' of jazz solos. Some of Dizzy Gillespie's solos in print looked as though a fly with ink on its feet had crawled across the paper! Of course, he played just what came into his head - leaving us poor blokes trying to figure out what he'd left behind afterwards. I managed to grasp quite a lot of it. Funnily enough, talking about transcripts, there's a friend of mine in New Orleans who writes to me quite regularly. He's got all my records, apparently, and has transcribed some of my own solos, which he sent to me. And I couldn't read any of them!

Around this time - 1946, maybe 1947 - I started going round to 'The Dairy' in Denmark Street, otherwise known as 'Tin Pan Alley', where all the music publishers had their offices. Everybody used to go and get a cup of tea at 'The Dairy' and all the publishers would go there, as well as the song pluggers - all of them Jewish. And, of course, I looked Jewish. In fact, I think they thought I was one of the 'Chosen Few', because they made a big fuss of me: "Kenny, my boy, how are you doing? Mazel tov, sonny Jim!" That was where I first met Billy Reed and Britain's first-ever diva, Dorothy Squires, who used to hire the London

Palladium to put on her concerts. Billy was in love with her; I can still see them holding hands. At that time Billy, an accordion player, had already written 'The Gypsy' and 'Tree in the Meadow'; he was a great songwriter. But he wouldn't let her sing any of his songs. She was always saying, "Bill, write a song for me." But he'd say, "No. Can't do it." Yes, he was a great writer; it's just that he couldn't write for her. I don't know why, he just had a thing about it. And later on, of course, she ditched him for Roger Moore!

### John:

*At the age of about 12 or 13 I really got into boogie woogie. I might've got into it even earlier if there'd been more records available in the shops. But, by a rare stroke of luck, I found a copy of 'Honky Tonk Train Blues' by blues pianist Meade Lux Lewis in a record shop in Palmers Green, and alongside it was Albert Ammons's aptly titled 'Shout for Joy'!*

*That pair of Parlophone 78s was the basis of what became a highly specialised record collection. I didn't go in for variety; the first thing I looked out for on a record label was the word 'boogie' in the title. That led to a few clangers - like 'Bumble Boogie': an orchestral fake boogie-woogie version of 'Flight of the Bumblebee', which I still keep as an example of what not to listen to! Later I looked out for records featuring blues pianists with colourful names. Pinetop Smith, Cow Cow Davenport and Speckled Red are three that spring to mind. I learnt most of their left-hand piano figures off by heart and then practised them for hours. After each practise session I felt almost as bombed-out as our old piano, but I was determined to get it right. If the rock 'n' roll craze had exploded onto the scene right then I'd have been in my element; after all, early rock 'n' roll, like jazz itself, has its roots firmly set in Negro rhythm and blues!*

*In about 1950, during one school lunch hour, I prised open the lock on the school piano with a nail file and gave vent to some eight-to-a-bar. Just two choruses of 'Honky Tonk Train Blues' were enough to bring the dinner-duty master shuffling in at top speed, waving his arms. I was tugged off the piano stool and the piano lid was slammed down and locked. The enthusiastic knot of pupils who'd gathered round me while I was playing thought this most unfair and made their presence felt. Others joined in, and to avoid a riot the master took the easy way out and unlocked the piano lid for me to continue playing. From that day on I performed regular lunch-hour boogie recitals to a horde of jiving youngsters.*

*Around that time came another turning point for me, when someone loaned me a copy of Mr Jelly Roll, a colourful biography of the jazz pianist Jelly Roll Morton. From that book I learned about the bordellos, rent parties, all-night rave-ups, dudes, girls, booze, brothels and all the seedy glamour of New Orleans at the turn of the century. For a newly graduated teenager who had led a sheltered life, it was probably too much information - but I swallowed it whole. From that moment on I was hooked. And that, Yer Honour, is how I became a traditional jazz fan some weeks before ever hearing a note of the music!*

### Kenny:

How did I get my first trumpet? Well, it was through my dad in - let me see - 1943. He'd given me £10, which was a lot of money then - two weeks' wages, in fact - to go and get this trumpet, which I'd seen in an advertisement in *Melody Maker*. In 1943 all available metal was being used to make guns and bullets and rifles, so a trumpet was hard to come by. It was a Saturday morning and, although I was only 13 years old, I took the tube all the way from Gants Hill to Kenton in Middlesex with £10 in my hands. But journeys don't mean much to kids, do they? Especially if they're on the trail of something they want. Anyway, I arrived there - I'd already phoned the bloke to say I wanted to buy the trumpet - and knocked at his door.

He opened it and said, "You'd better come in. There's been an accident."

15

"What's the matter?" I asked.

"The trumpet's broke," he replied.

"What do you mean broke?" I asked.

And - I swear this is true - he said, "I was having one last blow on it last night and my wife got so fed up with the racket I was making that she grabbed it and hit me over the head with it!"

I took a look and saw it was bent sideways - the whole trumpet bell.

Anyway, he continued, "You can have it for £8 if you like."

I thought, I'm not coming all this way for nothing. I've GOT to have a trumpet. So I gave him my £8. After all, it was only about tuppence to go home on the tube and now I had £2 change for Dad - and I had a mouthpiece. So I got hold of my trumpet, pushed it against the side of a tree and bent it straight. Talk about brute force and ignorance. And I went down the road blowing it right away! I'd been blowing a bugle in the Sea Cadets since I was 12 or 13, so I knew how to blow. I had an embouchure. But it was a bad one, because instead of teaching me to make sounds by tonguing behind the teeth I was told to spit into the mouthpiece, which is the worst thing to tell a trumpet player.

Anyhow, I had a mate - Ron Rudman, his name was - and soon there were four or five of us all with instruments. Ron played the piano a bit - just the melody with the odd bing-bong in the bass. I think he would rather have blown the bugle, but to begin with there wasn't one to spare. However, when I got my trumpet he took over my bugle. In fact, all of us had come out of the Sea Cadets, all messing about with different instruments. And this would've been about 1944. One of them, Alan Froom, had a side drum with brushes. His mum ran a café, I remember. Another bloke, John Meddiman, had an alto-saxophone and he could play the drums a bit, too. And there was me with my trumpet blasting out 'Come to the Cookhouse Door' or something like that. Anyhow, we had this little band and we learned about four tunes - just on the saxophone, trumpet, piano and snare drum - and we used to play around the local youth clubs. One of them was in Perryman's Farm in Ilford, and opposite there was a Dr Barnado's home where the girls used to live. Of course, they came across to the dance. We played our four tunes over and over again and nobody ever complained.

Later, the other three players all joined the Merchant Navy. You see, after de-mob in 1945 you could join the Merchant Navy as a steward or whatever. So they did, and that was the end of the band. John Meddiman went to South America, then on to Australia, though now he's back in England and keeps threatening to come and see me. But he never turns up. Alan Froom went to South Africa and stayed there, and Ron Rudman went to New Zealand and ended up on an island in the Bay of Auckland, as a postmaster. Funnily enough, I met him again a couple of years ago, just before he died. I wouldn't have minded joining the Merchant Navy myself. One of my brothers had been in the navy - gone to Africa and so forth. And in those days the only way you could see the world was in the Forces; you couldn't afford to go anywhere on your own. So I wouldn't have minded doing that. But all of my brothers had had enough of the war and the Forces and wouldn't let me go!

So now I had the trumpet and I got a tutor book. But I wanted to play tunes straight away rather than learn to play the trumpet the long way round. So what I did - and a lot of people do this - I'd hear the tune in my head and I'd just write down the valve fingerings. The first tune I notated like this was 'Darktown Strutter's Ball', which is open (in other words, no valves are pushed down); then valves 1 and 2, open again, 1 and 2, open again, and so on. I had a whole list of tunes written down like that, by the valve fingerings. I learned them just by trial and error. Then I started to try to read music, but I wasn't much good at it at the time. I used to use my ear more than anything else, you see, and once I'd heard the tune I could more or less play it. I haven't got perfect pitch - I can't hear a note and say, "That's a B-flat", for example - but I've got what they call 'relative pitch', so I can pick up a tune very easily.

My very first gig was with the Victor Hayes band. Victor was a drummer who worked in the Barking area, playing all the usual semi-pro gigs with their waltzes, quicksteps and foxtrots. I didn't know much about what was going on, but he said, "I've got a saxophone player, bass, drummer and pianist, and all we do is play tunes. Sit here …." And that was it. No trombones or anything, no luxuries. Anyway, he took me along in his car, which ran on gas bags - you'd fill them from the gas cooker. It's lucky no one ever dropped a match! Anyhow, we arrived at Wanstead Flats. On the flats they had an anti-aircraft post, fully equipped with rockets, and they used to hold dances there, too. So we got on the stage - no one had arrived yet - and I started to get nervous. Sod this for a game of soldiers, I thought. But Victor said, "You've got to stay - you're the only trumpet player we've got," to which I replied, "All right, but I'm not sitting on the stage - people can see me. I'll sit in the wings and play." And this is absolutely true, I swear. A few years ago two ladies came up to me and said, "Did you used to play at Wanstead Flats? At the Royal Artillery Unit? And did you play trumpet? Because we were at that dance and we could hear a trumpet but we couldn't see anybody playing it. And, in fact, you were very good." I got 15 shillings for that job, I remember - not bad!

By that time, I suppose, the word had got around about me as a young trumpeter. Anyhow, when I was about 17 I started to take it a little more seriously. I went to Phil Parker, who had a brass studio in Dansey Place off Shaftesbury Avenue; he was the best-known trumpet teacher in London at the time. He had two sons, one of whom went to Canada, and the other stayed in

London and became a very well known teacher himself. Both sons were excellent trumpet players; they were young men then, but Phil Parker was an old man. He had only one tooth in his head, yet he was one of those players that used a non-pressure method. He'd hang a trumpet on a piece of string and, with his hands behind his back, he'd blow an altissimo top C. He taught me something that I've passed on to so many kids, even though I don't use it myself now: you mustn't use pressure when you put the trumpet mouthpiece on your lips, because it sends the blood away and stifles the muscles and the notes won't come. So Phil designed a small stand made from a piece of wood, with a little ledge on which he put the trumpet for you to blow. So if you used pressure, you'd push the trumpet away. I used a book instead to try the same thing.

So Phil was the one who taught me the 'non-pressure' way of playing. But I forgot about all that later, when it came to real playing in a live situation. A couple of drinks and away you go. You can't practise once you're on stage; you've got to do it automatically.

### John:

*I was about 15 when I first saw and heard a live jazz band. It was at our local youth club and Terry Lightfoot's band was playing. Terry was a couple of years older than me, but I knew him by sight, as he'd attended the same primary school as me. So did his brother Paddy, who was my age and a friend of mine. Paddy was the banjoist in Terry's band at that time (and in the years to come would join the Kenny Ball Band on banjo/guitar).*

*I was impressed by the musicians in the band - all pupils of Enfield Grammar - and, above all, by the trombonist, John Pickard, who had a swashbuckling style that to me seemed the very essence of jazz. That's the posh way of putting it. What I was really thinking was that playing boogie piano was all very well, but waving a trombone slide around looked to be an even surer way of getting noticed by girls! (One of these days I might do a survey among the jazzmen of our era to establish just how many of us started out with nothing else on their minds than the pure and noble aim of creating jazz music, and how many had other aims on their minds, too!)*

*Pickard took his first solo, letting fly with a lavatorial rasp that rattled the windows and sounded, to my inexperienced ears, very much like my American jazz idol of the time, Kid Ory. I could do that, I thought. Of course, Pickard was one up on me, seeing as he owned a trombone and I didn't!*

*I solved that problem by joining my school orchestra. After some initial sparring, the music teacher and I struck a bargain: if I promised not to pollute the symphonic mood with my 'jungle nonsense' (word had got around about my jazz antics, and he was no jazz fan!) I could have the loan of the school trombone for an indefinite period and take my place in the school orchestra just as soon as I had learned how to play it.*

*That afternoon I left school rather furtively, with a long canvas bag tucked under my arm. Passers-by were curious, and how could I blame them? I must've looked like a poacher carrying a sack of dead ferrets in rigor mortis.*

*My first attempt at obtaining a sound out of the school trombone produced a strangled moan reminiscent, I would imagine, of a distressed cow giving birth to a two-headed calf. I was both surprised and delighted. But from then on it was all downhill: pianissimo led to fortissimo and then to complete frustration. After all, anyone could make noises like that. Granted, you could do it much louder with the aid of a trombone, but the effort was hardly worth it. Weeks passed, during which I felt obliged to stall the music teacher when he nagged at me to come to orchestra rehearsals. I wasn't quite ready yet, I would reply. "Still on page two of the manual, sir. But practice makes perfect, doesn't it?"*

*Perhaps it does - though not in my case. One of my problems was that I couldn't make head nor tail of sheet music. All those quavers, triplets or whatever, mounted on staves, looked about as accessible as barbed-wire fences. Not having the patience or will to get myself tangled up in No Man's Land, I decided to take a short cut.*

*I put the manual away, placed a Louis Armstrong record on the turntable and rasped duets along with trombonist Kid Ory. With my contribution, Armstrong's Hot Five temporarily became the Hot Six - and sounded the worse for it!*

### Kenny:

Let me see: it was about 1947, I suppose, when I met Ted Truman, a smashing chap who played saxophone. He had a harelip, so he'd stick the mouthpiece in the side of his mouth. It used to look as if he was blowing it out of his earhole!

He was ever such a nice chap; a decent man and sensitive to the extreme. He'd been very fond of his wife, I remember, and she'd died about 10 years earlier, and whenever he spoke about her he'd burst into tears; I mean really cry his heart out. He just couldn't control his emotions. Anyway, he took me under his wing.

Ted ran a band at a place called Collaro's in Barking. Sounds like a club, but it's not. Collaro's was a factory that made record players, and I used to work there. I only took a job there because they'd got a band that was short of a trumpet player. I hardly used to do any actual work, I must be honest. But every lunchtime we played in the factory canteen. Collaro's was a big company, with about 400 employees. And we used to play an hour's programme every day, which meant I was off an hour early and didn't go back till an hour later, so by the time I'd done a bit of work half the day had gone.

### John:

*I was not having much luck with the school trombone. Its slide used to jam up regularly and my well-meaning but ill-advised attempts to cure it with oil, soap, Vaseline and Blacklead only made matters worse.*

21

*Eventually, after a thorough examination, I diagnosed its malady as 'warping of the prong'. Moderate traction, I decided, was all that was needed.*

*I placed the inner slide across my knee and pressed down at both ends, upon which the slide abruptly folded like an elbow joint, cracking open at the point of stress. Like a surgeon confronted with a patient about to expire on his operating table, my reactions were instantaneous. After straightening the slide to near normal I applied Sellotape to the gaping wound. It would've been kinder, I know now, to have put the instrument out of its misery there and then by chucking it in the dustbin. It was the darkest day thus far in my short trombone-playing life, but I was determined not to get downhearted.*

*I still had a trombone, and I was going to use it; even though there was now little chance I would ever master the slick breath-and-slide control advocated in my brand-new Tommy Dorsey tutorial. How could I tackle such refinements when I was permanently in combat with a hostile armful of brass tubes? What I was doing bore little relation to music, though it was certainly getting closer to the music hall turn my dad said I was cut out for.*

*One day the slide jammed up completely, so that trying to shift it was like having a speculatory tug on Excalibur in the Stone. Very likely this was due to a chemical reaction caused by the various cosmetic treatments to which I had subjected it over the previous months. Unwittingly, I may well have stumbled upon the formula for superglue decades before its time. It was a nuisance; but, having not had too much success with trombone playing, I didn't look on it as a complete disaster.*

*In a few short weeks I would be leaving school for good, so I packed up my troubles in that old canvas bag and pretended it had never happened. Meanwhile, I went back to being the school's resident jazzer. My 'fans' had located a spare school piano standing unguarded in an annex and were pestering me to give a new series of lunchtime boogie recitals. I was happy to oblige, but the dinner-duty schoolmaster that day was certainly no fan of mine. Slamming the piano lid shut on me in amputatory fashion, he informed me that pianos were designed for more wholesome things - music, for example - and awarded me a detention. As I could still count all ten of my fingers, this seemed a small price to pay, so each day thereafter I prised the lock on that piano and played boogie until caught, as it were, red-handed. My stubbornness gained me a place in the school's underground hall of fame, but it also provoked the teaching staff into raising the stakes. Before long I was receiving more detentions than I could serve out in a lifetime. Every Monday morning I was notified of the surplus that had been carried over from the previous week. It was like doing time with accrued interest.*

*I kept on pounding away at the piano during the dinner hour because I enjoyed playing to a captive audience - except that when school ended our roles were reversed: the audience could enjoy their freedom while the piano player became the captive. I must've had a dozen or more nail files confiscated during this period. One of the younger teachers, a jazz fan himself, used to hang around the piano grinning and tapping his feet throughout the dinner hour. Afterwards, without a trace of shame, he would award me my customary pair of detentions - but that's showbiz! And the perks made up for everything: at long last I found I was attracting the attention of girls. A whole new vista was opening up.*

*In hindsight, I would say that I didn't make the most of it. I was handicapped by a lack of experience: a fairly general state of affairs in those innocent times - at least in grammar schools like ours. In 1951 there were no sex lessons, video nasties, drugs or trendy teachers. AIDS was still a generation away and VD was no concern of ours unless it was someone's initials. The worst that could happen was 'getting a girl into trouble', the penalties for which were unmentionable. That problem remained academic, too, as all the peaches-and-cream young maidens in our school were united in a bond of chastity.*

**Kenny:**
I started getting real results on the trumpet when I came out of the Army. That was in 1950 and I'd been in for two years: for

the first six months marching over hills and down dales between Hythe and Folkestone in the freezing winter as part of the Royal West Kent Regiment, then 18 months spent in Germany. They tried to make me an electrician without any training whatsoever; just put me in a factory and told me to get on with it. As an electrician, to be honest, I was completely useless. After all, I was only 18 years old and normally people would serve a five- or six-year apprenticeship to do that. They gave me just three months to learn all about the electrics on vehicles and plants.

I always had my trumpet with me. When I got to Germany there was a pianist playing the usual bing-bong and a drummer, whom I met again in Gloucester just recently. So we had a little band and we used to play in the sergeants' mess and the officers' mess. One little thing I used to do was to write to the BBC radio show, *Forces' Favourites*. My request for Bunny Berigan's 'I Can't Get Started' was played twice and even Dizzy Gillespie's 'Things to Come'. Then they had a radio talent competition coming out of the BFN studios in Hamburg, so I went and had a blow - I had no fear at all back in those days. In Germany I was stationed with a group called the LAD (Light Aid Detachment), part of REME (Royal Electrical and Mechanical Engineers), which involved picking up vehicles that had crashed, repairing them, and even hosing out dead bodies on occasion. I also did shift work as a driver. But this was a funny thing. Of course we'd had no meat for years; it was still rationed in England. But they used to give us carte blanche to go into the cookhouse, because we were on duty all night. So we used to go down to a German village nearby. It had been very well bombed during the war, so we British weren't exactly the most popular visitors, but I was so naïve - I thought everybody was wonderful. On Saturday mornings I'd go down with a few German marks in my sweaty little hands and queue up with the locals at the butcher's shop to get a pork chop to cook up in the cookhouse.

So finally, when I came home on leave, I remember playing at the Barking Town Hall. There was an accordion player and a juggler, and the theme was 'Young Man with a Horn' -because of the film of that title starring Kirk Douglas and Doris Day, which was very popular at the time. They had a talent competition and I won it.

As for British trumpeters at the time, I liked Humphrey Lyttelton's playing - very direct. But, of the Americans back then, my favourite trumpet player was probably Bunny Berigan. And then Harry James was a big influence in my life, with tunes like 'Boo-Woo' and 'Woo Woo' - they were terrific. I really love that sort of sound, with the growl mute. Funnily enough, I used to play both of those routines with Billy Penrose, the piano player with Sid Phillips' band.

I didn't get into Louis Armstrong until about 1949 and that was when I heard the Town Hall Concert on 78rpm. That knocked me dead! But, funnily enough, I couldn't find any Louis Armstrong records at that time. You couldn't just go into a shop and get any record you wanted. I later found a French 10-inch album with some of the Hot Fives on it. One of the tracks was 'Cornet Chop Suey' and another was 'Potato Head Blues', which I learned note for note. I recorded it on my second album, *Kenny Ball and His Jazzmen*.

# 3
# GOING PRO

*John:*

*I left school in 1952, never having played in my school orchestra, nor having learned to read music. So while I was saving up to buy my very own trombone I set about teaching myself basic harmony the hard way, by working out chords on our old piano with the aid of* The George Formby Banjo Tutor *(price one shilling and sixpence from Woolworths - tremendous value!) Within a few weeks I was faking Kid Ory phrases on imaginary 'air trombone'! Just as well, then, that I was able to afford a 'new' second-hand trombone before the men in white coats could be summoned!*

*I found out, much later, that Ken and I had followed uncannily similar paths after leaving school. Like Ken, I got a job in an advertising agency. The firm was Masius and Ferguson - which coincidentally was a couple of floors higher in the very same building in Berkeley Square as J. Walter Thompson, the firm that Ken had started out with nine years earlier.*

*I, too, went to Phil Parker's brass studios in Dansey Place, Soho, where Ken had also gone for lessons. And it was Phil Parker who managed to cure me of the same technical problem that Ken had when starting to play trumpet: of 'spitting' into the mouthpiece instead of using the tongue against the back of your front teeth.*

*When I went into the Army on National Service I was selected - conned is a better word - to play piano in a dance band quartet. The bandleader was a regular army corporal with plenty of savvy. We played regularly at gigs in the sergeants' mess, which I was led to believe was the number one nightspot in our sector of Aldershot. To persuade me to*

26

*play at these functions, the corporal would remind me of the fee I would be getting, and the privileges. The main privilege, as far as I could make out, was an amnesty with the regimental police after lights out - which was of no great benefit to me as I'd far rather have been fast asleep in my bunk than tottering around the parade ground at midnight, knowing I'd be up again at dawn.*

*But at least the gig money was something to look forward to. From what I could gather, the kitty was getting fairly substantial - though exactly how much was in it remained a mystery. "Pay you at the end of next week," repeated the corporal each time I queried why the cash hadn't yet changed hands. One week I was not asked to play at the sergeants' mess. The corporal wasn't around, but I was assured by his smirking deputy that everything had been taken care of and that the gig money had been posted on - not to my address, as it turned out. The 'posting' had been the corporal's, and our quartet's fees had accompanied him to his new address in Singapore!*

### Kenny:

Later on, of course, I did learn to read music - with Sid Phillips. And I played in a couple of dance bands, including The Orchettes - a very good band run by Frank Ditcham. They used to play all the Gerry Mulligan pieces. We did a few *Melody Maker* competitions and I managed to win the Best Trumpeter accolade a few times. Frank and Joyce Ditcham are still my best friends. That was in the early '50s - before I joined Sid, and around the time I was working with trombonist Charlie Galbraith's band.

I was with Charlie Galbraith from 1951 to '52 and I think it was originally Dave Jones who introduced me to him. At that time Charlie had a two-trumpet front line. The sound we were after was that of Lu Watters & the Yerba Buena Jazz Band, who started the jazz revival in San Francisco. Yerba Buena was the original name for San Francisco - I think it means 'New Earth'.

27

I loved that band, made up of really good players, with Turk Murphy, Bob Scobey, Bob Helm and Wally Rose on piano. The band was a copy of the great King Oliver band, but they used to have a lot of original material, and of course they had a great singer, Clancy Hayes, who wrote his own material - and it was great stuff. They recorded for the Good Time Jazz label.

I really liked the sound, because with two trumpets you could play some great harmonies. In Charlie's band Bill Thompson - a lovely trumpet player who passed away in 2009 - played first trumpet and I played second. (Somewhere I've got a programme of all of us at the Jazz Band Jubilee at the Royal Albert Hall - so we did play some big places.)

Back then, in the early 1950s, I sometimes used to sub for Freddie Randall, who really was a marvellous Dixieland trumpet player; certainly one of the two or three best in Britain at that time. But Freddie used to get a bad lip occasionally and would ask me to stand in for him. As a result, his agent started booking me on my own. But he had some funny ideas: when he was talking to me about having a band of my own he was saying, "You should get flutes, violins, that sort of thing," which, of course, wasn't my vision at all.

Anyhow, in the meantime Sid Phillips' agent asked him if he knew of a trumpet player that could fill the soloist's job with Sid's band and he recommended me. I could hardly read a note of music, but I joined Sid anyhow in late 1953. Billy Penrose, Sid's pianist, was the most lovely of chaps. When you were on tour in those days you used to have to double up in a twin-bedded room, because you couldn't afford one on your own, so Bill and I used to share a room. He'd turn up ready to get on the band bus, going to somewhere like Nottingham or Sheffield, with his suitcase and his dress suit already on. Then at the other end we'd get out, find the digs, and if there was a bathroom available I'd get my dressing gown and say, "Are you getting washed?" And he'd say, "No, I had a wash before I came out." And in his suitcase there was nothing but beer - no shirts, no underpants; he was already wearing everything! Remember, I was only about 23 and I didn't drink at all in those days. But Billy would do the gig, come back to the digs, take off his trousers and go to bed in his underpants! We were together for quite some time, Bill and I.

I was with Sid twice as a matter of fact. I left for a bit to work with Norman Cave's band, and then I had my own band for a short time, before returning to Sid's band in 1954 for a couple of years. In 1954 I got married to my first wife Betty and we were together for 26 years.

### John:

*I didn't know Ken at that time, mainly because he was a Dixieland player and I belonged to the beard-and-sandals brigade: playing so-called purist New Orleans jazz, popularised by the likes of Ken Colyer. British jazz was much more compartmentalised back then. The 'Trads' and the 'Modernists' in particular just didn't get on. Their clothing was different; their style of dancing was different. And the symbol marking this difference was the saxophone: loved by the modernists; loathed by the Trads. It was the fans - certainly not the musicians - that decided these things. Those of us who were around at the time will never forget when Bruce Turner played his first concert with the Humphrey Lyttelton band at Birmingham Town Hall in 1953. Just because Bruce played alto saxophone, a group of Humph's more traditionalist fans unfurled a large banner reading: 'GO HOME DIRTY BOPPER'.*

*My first paid gig was in 1953, with trumpeter Trevor Williams's Jazz Band in a cellar in Gerrard Street, Soho, where much of the time the band played to itself while the clientele fought it out with chairs and bottles on the tiny space laughingly called the dance floor! We also played at the temple of British trad: Ken Colyer's 51 Club, a cramped cellar just behind Leicester Square tube station. That club was presided over by a large lady with a glass eye, who would dispense free bottles of beer in her kitchen to the musicians and their hangers-on.*

*While on the subject of glass eyes, it's just struck me that in those days there seemed to be an above-average percentage of folks around the trad jazz scene that sported this fashion accessory: Bob Wallis, for one. He was a trumpet player and bandleader, who on one hilarious occasion 'accidentally' dropped his glass eye in a bucket of winkles shared by a dozen musicians and had to wait until someone won the lucky dip before he could 'see' again. Another was Cyril Keepfer, Trevor Williams' clarinettist, who once stayed overnight at my parents' home and apologised to me for taking his eye out and leaving it on top of our old piano before turning in. It was a pretty uncomfortable night, as I recall. Our piano had by then been moved into my bedroom, and to create a bit of space in that tiny room my single bed had been put away and we each lay on a narrow mattress on either side of that aged instrument. During the night one of us must've nudged the piano in our restlessness, for I vaguely remember hearing a melodic plonk as Cyril's glass eye rolled off the top and hit middle C. The next morning we spent about 20 minutes rummaging around on the floor for it - even then our cat found it first and batted it out into the hall!*

### Kenny:

One of the first cars I had was when I was working with Charlie Galbraith Jazzmen down in South London. I didn't have it for long. Coming home one night, the bonnet flew off and I never saw it again. And I was nearly home when I ran over a poor bloody cat. All on that same night! It was a terrible night; an unlucky car, too - not to say an unlucky cat!

That wasn't all. It had an oil leak that stopped the dynamo, so all the lights would go out. Once, coming back from Leytonstone, I nicked - I'm sorry about this, Mr Policeman - I *borrowed* a light that I'd picked up off the road. It shone white on one side and red on the other. So I got my wife to sit on the back seat with her hand up in the air, holding this roadside light (which was full of paraffin!) with the red light shining towards the back and the white light shining to the front. And we drove all the way home like that and didn't get stopped, fortunately.

In the 1950s I built myself a car. It was an Austin 7 van originally, from around 1930, I think. It cost me about 25 quid. I took the body off, turned the chassis upside down and reversed the springs so it would have a very low centre of gravity. The engine had its compression raised, and I increased the head gasket to 7 as opposed to 5, using the valves with double springs to make it go faster. I wanted to put an Ashley body on it to make it a light sports car, because every young man in those days wanted a sports car. So I got the Ashley body, which cost about 50 quid, and I had a cousin who was an electrician, so he made me an electric 'loom' for 30 quid and we stuck it together. Then I built a space frame, which is the bodywork it sat on. I could only build it with angle iron, as I couldn't afford the aluminium, which probably made it weigh half a ton as opposed to 300lbs. I couldn't afford the metal to put in a floor, but I fitted two aircraft seats where the floor should've been. I managed to get a hood made, too, so in the end I had me a sports car.

Pat Mason was a wonderful chap and my piano player at the time (around 1952). We had a gig in Reading and we weren't sure how we were going to get there, So I told him, well, my car's going; it has no bottom underneath, but we've got seats. The only thing is, we'll have to push it to get it going because the starter motor won't work, and I couldn't afford one anyhow. Anyway, we got it going, and off we went to Reading. When we were halfway there it started piddling down with rain. Poor old Pat and I arrived at Reading jazz club with our arses completely soaked. We went in, did the gig - I think we got 30 bob each – and then got back in the car, started it up and drove all the way home. We were totally saturated by then and could've easily caught pneumonia.

So that was my experience with a car I built myself. It cost me £175 in all and I sold it for 175 quid too. I saw it running around Chelmsford about 10 years later.

### John:

*My first car was a sporty one, too: an MG J2, 1932 vintage. It'd looked rakish sitting in its previous owner's garage, with its gleaming grey and maroon paintwork, spoked wheels, sporty leather strap across its bonnet and spare wheel slung on the petrol tank at the rear. I'd saved up for months, and I paid £130 for it on the spot. But it became a casualty before I'd even driven it out of its former owner's garage: I managed to snap the half-shaft and then found it would take two months to have a new one specially cast, then get it fitted! During that time I'd go round to that garage most days and sit in the driving seat going, "Brrrm, brrrm." It was a sad business.*

*I then rented a garage closer to home, adjoining a bungalow belonging to an elderly lesbian couple. That lease came to an ignoble end when I backed out of their drive and knocked over their garden wall. The two ladies were most irate and refused to allow me back on their territory, so for a couple of weeks I parked my MG at the curb outside my home, pocketing the distributor head whenever I had to leave it for any length of time. I spent endless sunny afternoons happily polishing up the chrome and bodywork while whistling Louis Armstrong trumpet choruses.*

*I was not a natural sports car owner. My MG had a crash gearbox, which meant I'd need to learn a technique known as double-declutching. Fortunately, my pal Colin Smith, later to become Acker Bilk's trumpet player, was a real hard-core sports car fanatic, and he showed me how to do this poseur's trick with nifty bursts of loud revving.*

*It wasn't until towards the end of my first year of ownership that my MG began to show real signs of its great age. Nothing very significant at first; just a casual shedding of minor nuts, bolts, springs and suchlike along the highway, the loss of which seemed to have not the slightest effect on the car's performance. Now and again I would notice curls of black smoke issuing from behind the dashboard, but I learned how to put that right by giving the tangle of bare wiring under there a quick shake. On one occasion I shook the wiring a little too vigorously and my car burst into flames. This was embarrassing, as it happened on Highgate Hill during the rush hour, and furthermore I had an important passenger - Ted Morton, the boss of Jazzshows Promotions - sitting alongside. I immediately took the necessary action: switched off, disentangled the wires, and blew the smoke away. Then I turned to grin nonchalantly at my passenger, but his seat was empty. I spotted him striding briskly up the street about 30 yards away. "It's okay, thanks," he called back nervously in answer to my query. "I can walk from here - it's only a couple of miles."*

*Soon after that incident I sold my MG. I got what I'd paid for it, but shortly afterwards I had to give £10 back to the buyer. He'd driven only a couple of miles before the radiator detached itself and dropped out into the road!*

### Kenny:

In 1956 I joined Eric Delaney's big band. They were still very popular at the time and Eric had his own unique sound by using tuned timpani in his arrangements. He had some pretty big hits, too –'Oranges and Lemons' was one. John Dankworth reminded me that on his own hit record 'Experiments with Mice' (a sort of parody of how famous big bands would've played 'Three Blind Mice') Eric's was the only British band to get their own slot, alongside Stan Kenton, Benny Goodman, Sauter-Finegan, and so on. That's how big he was.

As I said, I still couldn't read music very well, but I took Eric's book home in advance and learned it, you see. Why did Eric hire me when I wasn't really a big-band player? Well, the Traditional jazz movement was getting going and I think Eric thought it would be good to have a Dixieland-based musician in the band. Plus, he was a lovely chap, and we're still very good friends today!

A lot of funny things happened to that band. One of our arrangements was 'Roamin' in the Gloamin'' and Eric - who was very fond of special effects - had a backdrop put up for a gig in Liverpool. It ran on direct current and was a sort of weather effect, with clouds moving steadily across, rain coming down, and so on - all very suitable for the gloamin'. Well, one night we looked around while we were playing and noticed that the clouds were absolutely racing across the sky at high speed and the rain was going up instead of down. The polarity on the machine had reversed somehow, and needless to say the whole band was in hysterics!

Another arrangement that Eric had was the 'Sailors' Hornpipe' - a very up-tempo, tricky number - and for this one he used to set up two 15-inch guns at the side of the trumpet section. On a set cue, which we all knew about of course, there'd be a controlled explosion at the side of the stage - really a big cracker in a dustbin - and the guns would both emit a puff of smoke. It was all very carefully arranged and synchronised, and it was very effective. However, on this particular night we saw the smoke coming out of the guns, but there was no accompanying bang - not even a rumble. Anyhow, we finished the arrangement and on came the lady singer that Eric had at the time. Her number was a very graceful version of 'Baubles, Bangles and Beads'. Well, you can guess what happened. Right in the middle of her performance there was this unbelievable "Wallop!" - a huge explosion. The poor girl jumped out of her skin, of course, and the whole band was in hysterics again.

Having said that, the atmosphere in the band wasn't too good a lot of the time. Big band players often were very cliquish and not very nice at all in my opinion. I had a clique of three mates, including the lead alto, Des Lumsden - a very fine musician - plus the pianist and bassist, and we were like the 'Gang of Four'. But the other players, including a trumpeter that I won't name because he was a total bastard to me, used to gang up on Eric and sometimes on me, too. Eric had me doing rock 'n' roll tunes at one point - including Elvis' 'Blue Suede Shoes' - and when we were down at Southampton one night I had my shirt ripped off by all the shrieking girl fans. In the end, Eric had had enough - and me, too. The big bands were dying anyhow; rock was coming in. Finally, he said, "Blow it! I'll start a small group," which he did - a very good one with Tony Fisher on trumpet and Jimmy Skidmore on tenor. And he went up to Blackpool and did very well up there.

I started broadcasting around this time, too. One of the first occasions was in 1956, if I remember rightly. It was the BBC Jazz Club and Charlie Galbraith was with me. I'd started off with his band, but now it had turned into my band, because I was starting to get better known, you see. I had Sid Phillips' bass player, dear old Pat Mason, on piano and Johnny Welling on drums, who was great. And the band sounded really good. Dill Jones had a solo piano spot to himself and the announcer was guitarist Ken Sykora. That was before I joined Terry Lightfoot, of course - and round about the time I met John Bennett.

### John:

*I'd joined the Terry Lightfoot Band back in late 1956. A year later Terry was looking for a new trumpet player for his band and he asked me to go along with him to listen to Kenny Ball (a name that at that time meant nothing to me). That night Kenny's band was appearing at his local jazz club - the Greyhound pub in Chadwell Heath. Terry and I drove there and found a vantage point at the back of the room where we could see everything that went on. While keeping one eye on the twirling frilly petticoats of the dancers (the girls, that is!) I noticed that, unlike in the*

*Lightfoot band, Kenny's front-line musicians remained seated during ensembles. Very posh, I thought. Then Kenny stood up to take his first solo. He let rip with such an utterly amazing volley of notes that to this day I can still recall how the hairs on the back of my neck stood on end. I gaped at Lightfoot and said, "Wow!" Soon after, Kenny joined the Lightfoot band.*

### Kenny:

When John Bennett came down to the Chadwell Heath jazz club with Terry Lightfoot in the late 1950s I was playing with John Potter and his Chicagoans, which had sort of become Kenny Ball and the Chicagoans. John came up with his trombone and sat in. Well, John played this fantastic, mellifluous sound. He was playing in the style of Cutty Cutshall (the trombonist with the Eddie Condon band in the USA). It was exactly the type of trombone playing I admire.

Later, when I was working with Terry Lightfoot's band, I got to know John better. John was a very handsome chap - the rotten swine! He had this Elvis Presley quiff, which attracted the girls. Later still, when our band got started, I used John's good looks to our advantage. When we were a bit tiddly and having a laugh I'd get John to do an Elvis Presley impersonation.

After a few months I fell out with Terry over the policy of the band. There was a bit of finger pointing and I left. I wanted to get my own band going and get my own sound. After being with the Lightfoot band I felt I'd got to move forward. John said, "Well, if you're leaving I'll join you." I replied, "You're welcome, mate," and within months we'd got going.

We used to meet at John's home. He was still living with his parents then, and his mum used to supply the tea and biscuits. That was where we planned the future Jazzmen. We shared the same musical interests: the Eddie Condon Band, the Hackett-Teagarden recordings like 'Coast Concert' and trombonist

Wilbur de Paris's band, which not a lot of people know about these days. We aimed to fit our style somewhere among those styles.

John has been one of the most loyal friends I ever could've wished for. He stuck with me through thick and thin when we were just starting out and staying in those horrible places: bed and breakfast and transport cafes. John never complained at all. Never. We've been together now for 50-odd years and it don't seem a day too long. I think the world of him and his family: his wife, Ann, and their children. God bless them all. And John's mum and dad gave us plenty of encouragement in those very early days. His dad died soon after the band started out, which was a terrible blow - he never knew how successful the band was to become.

# 4
# THE KENNY BALL BAND

*Kenny:*

In October 1958 John Bennett, pianist Colin Bates and I all decided to leave Terry's band and go out on our own. We decided to call the band Kenny Ball's Dixielanders, because we all loved the sort of music we'd heard on albums like *Coast Concert* by Bobby Hackett and Jack Teagarden and *Coast to Coast* by Eddie Condon and his double front-line band. Just marvellous. Dave Jones came with us and so did banjoist Johnny Potter. We also had Brian Prudence on bass, but he was called up for National Service soon after. So we recruited Colin Purbrook alongside Colin Bates. Both were terrific pianists, but they agreed to share piano duties until we could get a 'proper' bass player. So for a while Colin Purbrook doubled on bass when Colin Bates was playing piano, and Bates doubled on tuba when Purbrook took over on piano.

Our agent was the great double bassist Jack Fallon, a Canadian fellow who also played country and western fiddle. He had his own agency, the Cana Variety Agency. Jack took us on, John and I. He said he would get us, I think, £6,000 for the first six months if we signed up with him for four years. Well we did. We just about made it, and he signed us on. And June was our secretary, who managed all our bookings. She eventually married Alan Elsdon, the trumpet player. She was a lovely lady - she still is. But Alan, unfortunately, is now seriously ill.

In April 1959 Jack got us a residency at the Storyville Club in Frankfurt. But this was a problem, because several of the band had day jobs and Johnny Potter, Dave Jones, Brian Prudence and Colin Purbrook all decided they couldn't go.

**John:**

*Colin Purbrook's exit from the band was quite dramatic. A few days before we were due to set off for Germany the band had been invited to a house party in Liverpool, which, as was usual in those days, turned into a fairly boisterous shindig. At some point during the festivities we realised that Colin wasn't present and hadn't been for some time. One or two of us remembered seeing Colin stagger upstairs to a second-floor bathroom, but no one had seen him return. It took a few moments for the implications to penetrate our sozzled brains, after which, with the over-enthusiastic concern of the inebriated, we all rushed upstairs like the Keystone Cops and battered down the bathroom door. The room was empty, the window was wide open and the curtains were flapping in the dawn breeze. Apparently Colin had taken it into his head to clamber out, shin down the drainpipe and vanish into the night. In the years to come we occasionally received reports from people who claimed they'd met up with Colin in various corners of the world, but it was not until 20 years later that we ran into Colin again - at a BBC radio studio, where he was fronting a modern jazz trio. In true British stiff-upper-lipped fashion I greeted Colin with a handshake and didn't enquire about his absence during the missing two decades. Nor did he volunteer an explanation. Sadly Colin died in 1999, so now we'll never know.*

**Kenny:**

We took along a clarinettist called Alan Cater and banjoist Dickie Bishop (who'd previously worked with Chris Barber, so was an old hand at the game). Then in Frankfurt we picked up bassist Vic Pitt, who was with me all through the trad years. Vic had started his career at only 17 with a skiffle group, the City Ramblers, led by Russell Quaye - they were quite famous at the time. He'd already done one month with another band in

Frankfurt and stayed on to do another excellent month with us. He was about half the size of his bass, but could he play!

For all of us Frankfurt was good, hard training - as it would be for The Beatles in Hamburg a few years later. The band really started to improve. But, of course, all of us were flat broke. In Frankfurt we used to go to eat in a place that offered bean soup at one deutschmark and that was what we used to live on. We were earning hardly anything, but I have to say the band was terrific and Germany really opened things up for us. When we got back to England Dave Jones decided to throw in his day job and rejoin the band permanently. That was another bit of luck, as then the band really got going. Pretty soon we were getting a lot of attention - particularly from Steve Race, who was very well known as a BBC 'Voice of Jazz' and a journalist, as well as a very fine piano player. It was quite a surprise at the time, as Steve was really more linked to modern jazz in Britain.

*John:*

*A typical suburban London jazz club in those days would be a small and rather staid ballroom with a high stage and a revolving mirrored ball hanging from the ceiling on which a spotlight played, sending flurries of luminous polka dots whizzing around the walls. Sometimes, to add 'atmosphere', the room lighting would be veiled with coloured crêpe paper, which dimmed things down to wartime blackout-regulation level. Members of the audience that arrived early for the weekly jazz session would sit along the walls and gaze sheepishly at their opposite numbers across the room. Before the band appeared on stage the mood would be muted and rather formal, like the opening of an end-of-term school dance. That was hardly surprising, as the strongest beverage obtainable in many of these places was undiluted orange squash. But as soon as the session got under way the place would come alive, with dancers loping about the floor performing weird variations on current jive routines, while the bystanders stomped and cheered. At the interval there would be a general exodus to the pub up the road, usually with the bandleader heading the joyful procession like Moses leading his flock to the backside of the desert.*

*Harrow Jazz Club, sited in the local British Legion Hall, was characteristic of this type of trad jazz venue. One evening, in May 1959, Steve Race arrived there early to catch a session by the Kenny Ball Band. Beforehand, while chatting to Kenny, he admitted that his taste in jazz was for a rather more modern and sophisticated sound than ours, but his wife liked to listen to Dixieland and anyway he didn't object to the occasional glass of orange squash. The band, having just returned from our month in Frankfurt, was match fit and on top form and the session, as I recall it, was one of our better ones. It so impressed Steve Race that he stayed longer than he'd planned and he was moved to write a highly flattering piece about the band in* **Melody Maker** *the following week. He expressed surprise that the Kenny Ball band was not currently available on record: "If the band can swing in a studio the way it does in a British Legion Hall, some bright recording company could have a new Barber band on its hands."*

*Encouraging as this sounded at the time, it soon became apparent that no bright recording company executive had seen fit to read* **Melody Maker** *that week, as there was no reaction to the article. Another year went by ...*

*Steve Race, extract from* **Melody Maker**, *23 May 1959*
*... Let's put it in a sentence: the Kenny Ball Jazzmen constitute one of the most exciting things on the current traditionalist scene. There is no weak link anywhere in the group. Trumpeter Kenny Ball himself blows a strong, toneful lead, and is a likeable leader. Trombonist John Bennett plays with the fire of Trummy Young, laced with flashes of Teagarden's technical facility, though his style is very much his own. Dave Jones (clarinet) produces driving sound without sacrificing the tone of his instrument. The three of them comprise a swinging, sympathetic front-line which would make*

*exciting listening, even without such a good rhythm section.*

*Along the back row sit Colin Bates (piano), Vic Pitt (bass), Dickie Bishop (banjo) and Tony Budd (drums), working genuinely as a team, and sometimes driving the band to a pitch of excitement which has to be felt to be believed.*

*Yes; this is a rave notice for a band which disproves all the modernists' pet theories about trad musicians …*

### Kenny:

We were now starting to make a big name on the jazz club circuit all around London and the city borders. It used to be called the 'Milk Round' and all the bands played it; pubs with their own halls like the Red Lion in Hatfield and Barnet Jazz Club, both of them run by Ken Lindsay, a well-known promoter for years - right into the late 1970s. Then there was Watford; British Legion Club, Harrow; The Cooks Ferry Inn, Edmonton; The Fleet Street Jazz Club at lunchtimes …

### John:

*… The Cherry Tree, Welwyn Garden City; The Fishmonger's Arms, Wood Green; Chislehurst Caves …*

### Kenny:

… The Tiger's Head, Catford; The Black Prince, Bexley; The Star, Croydon; The Royal Oak, Dagenham - oh, there were loads of suburban London clubs and all of them were always packed out. Once we broke the attendance record at Humphrey Lyttelton's old jazz club in the cellar at 100 Oxford Street, where we played to 680 people. How they got them all in I'll never know, and during the week leading up to that night we broke several box-office records playing to over 6,000 people. In fact, we were breaking records all over the place - but not really *making* any, apart from one EP in August 1959 on the Jazz

Collector label. We'd made the EP for Colin Pomeroy and it had a 13-minute version of the blues 'Baby Doll', which I'd really liked when I heard Humphrey Lyttelton do it. We still play that number. Of course, we were playing around England too; tons of club dates all through 1959. We were regularly at Liverpool.

### John:

*We played one weekend every month at the Mardi Gras Club in Mount Pleasant, near the Adelphi Hotel and not far from Liverpool's Lime Street station. Harry Ormisher was running it at that time. I remember it well, but memories are now all that's left - the building was flattened into a car park many years ago. The Mardi Gras had a low stage and a frayed backcloth depicting the New York skyline at midnight. There were several bars, a billiard room and wall-to-wall audiences. Our regular monthly visits to the Mardi Gras were lost weekends for one and all, and we needed the intervening weeks to recover. Our sessions there often used to culminate in a bizarre send-up of a rock 'n' roll number, during which Vic Pitt laid on his back on the stage still playing his bass, Colin Bates draped himself over the upright piano, shoes and socks removed, playing the keyboard with his toes, and the rest of us clowned, cavorted, swapped instruments and went generally berserk. Sessions at the Mardi would end in a grand finale: the band marching off stage to 'Didn't He Ramble', gathering followers as we waltzed through every door in the place - including the ladies' loo, which was always packed with hooting females. While in there the band was subjected to a weird fertility rite - over which a veil should be drawn, emerging some time later swathed in toilet rolls like Egyptian mummies. The session would end with the procession winding its way downstairs and out into the night.*

### Kenny:

Our drummer up to then had been ... let me see ... First was Tony Allen, who stayed for about a week, then we tried out Jimmy Garforth, and finally we went for Tony Budd. But then in the summer of 1959 Tony told us that he couldn't carry on; he was a family man and needed a regular income. He'd decided to set up his own window-cleaning business, which was a shame because he was a very good drummer. Fortunately, that same day Dickie Bishop encountered drummer Ron Bowden in a pub in Archer Street near the old Cy Laurie jazz club, where we were rehearsing. Ron was a bit older than the rest of us and had played with Chris Barber's band, as well as on Lonnie Donegan's huge hit 'Rock Island Line'. So he had quite a pedigree - and he stayed with us for 40 more years. A terrific drummer.

### John:

*Ron had left the Barber band only the previous year to open a restaurant in Brighton, but his new career hadn't got off to a good start. In fact his first, and only, year as a restaurateur was disastrous. Train strikes and a long period of bad summer weather hadn't helped, nor had Ron's lifelong addiction to betting shops. At one stage funds were so low that Ron was forced to keep customers waiting while he nipped out the back door to the local butcher's shop, where he used the proceeds from the previous order to buy food for the next. Eventually, the weather turned for the better, but by then it was too late - Ron's restaurant had folded and he was down on his uppers. Since then there had been one brief respite - a week's tour playing drums for green-haired rock singer Wee Willie Harris - but after that Ron was back once again on Archer Street, open to all offers.*

*Dickie and Ron returned to our rehearsal room, where Tony Budd was about to make his departure. Tony shook hands with Ron and, like drummers the world over, they conversed in 'Drummer's Cymbalese' - a secret language couched in paradiddles, flams, heads, Allen keys, mummy-daddies and other weird percussionistic terms. Then, while Tony packed away his drums, Ron set up his own kit, after which Tony made his last farewells and sped off to get busy with his leather and bucket. It was an efficient takeover; rather like a couple of Olympic relay athletes exchanging batons. We then carried on with our rehearsal almost as if nothing had happened. Changes of personnel don't usually work as smoothly as that!*

### Kenny:

In February 1960 we went back to play a second residency at the Storyville in Frankfurt. This time it wasn't so exciting. We'd been doing really well in England, so coming back was a bit of an anticlimax and we all felt a bit low. What was worse, we all had to stay in three adjoining rooms in digs run by a landlady called Frau Behrens. That Frau Behrens was a right so-and-so. She had a picture on the wall and we used to throw darts at it, thinking it was a portrait of Adolf Hitler - but it turned out to be a portrait of her dead husband.

### John:

*We spent our afternoons shivering in her unheated lounge, passing the time by chucking darts at that portrait. Frau Behrens was puzzled by the strange noises coming from her lounge but never managed to catch us in the act. Hearing her footsteps approaching, we hid the darts and would be reclining in armchairs apparently absorbed in detective novels by the time she stormed in demanding to know, "Vot is der schlapp, schlapp, schlapp noise I am hearing?" Our landlady seemed quite unaware of the rapidly deteriorating condition of her painting, which, having been peppered with darts, now gave her late husband the appearance of having sat for his portrait while suffering from terminal smallpox.*

*Once you'd checked in for the night, she'd lock all the doors so you couldn't get out again. One night Vic Pitt and I rebelled. We climbed out of a window - which was a feat in itself, even though it was a ground-floor window, as both of us were fairly legless by then. As I had the keys to the van, I suggested we hop in for a middle-of-the-night drive to see the sights of the Frankfurt suburbs. I hadn't the slightest idea where I was headed, and to make matters worse I was driving on the wrong side of the road. Soon the police flagged us down, and, realising we were from the UK, they asked for my passport. I didn't have it with me, so I gave them my English driving licence instead. They held it upside down for a bit, then let us off. Those were the days!*

### Kenny:

One night Dickie Bishop, who'd joined us on banjo after Johnny Potter left, was sharing a room with me. We both went to sleep, but then I was woken up by a sort of clapping sound. It was pitch-black and the noise went on and on. I thought, hello, someone's having one off the wrist, but then I put the light on and saw Dickie Bishop had gone to sleep with a lit cigarette in his hand. It had fallen onto his cotton underpants, and you know cotton burns slowly. But Dickie was still pissed and still fast asleep, with his gusset fizzing like an incendiary bomb, and was trying to put out the fire by slapping the burning bit. So there were odd funny moments. But it was depressing, especially as we'd been getting so big in England.

A lot of drinking went on, as over there we had to play from 8 p.m. until about 3 o'clock in the morning. Talk about slave labour. Dickie Bishop was a bit older than the rest of us, and in Frankfurt he used to drop off to sleep while he was actually playing; slowing up bit by bit until he came to a stop altogether. What a ...! Anyhow, he'd go to sleep and the band would carry on playing. Then we'd stop and suddenly he'd wake up and start playing again.

One night I turned round to have a go at him for all his snoozing and saw he wasn't there. He'd left the stand and gone missing and no one had seen him go. When the gig was over we drove round Frankfurt looking for him and eventually found him in a really horrible bar. He'd drunk about 12 beers and had then discovered he hadn't got the money to pay for them. Just before we arrived, the owner had sent for the police and Dickie, on the point of being handcuffed, had ordered the owner to call the British Consul. So we'd arrived just in the nick of time.

When we got back to England Dickie left the band for a while and Diz Disley took over until Dickie came back about six months later. That was in May 1960, but in the late autumn Dickie finally left for good, and Vic Pitt's brother, Tony, came in on guitar for a few weeks until Bill Dixon replaced him.

### *John:*

*We had quite a few changes around that time. Colin 'Barney' Bates left. 'Barney', the band's first pianist, was a gangly fellow whose shifty manner resembled that of an ex-schoolmaster with a murky past. He got his nickname from a stunt he used to play in the early days of the band. Pretending to be a down-and-out, he would solicit strangers on the street with the plea, "Spare a fag for old Barney?" Old Barney's performances were pretty convincing, and in those hard-up days a cigarette plus an occasional charitable half-crown were a useful supplement to his band income.*

*Barney was very absent-minded. Once, after a particularly heavy night, he woke up to find himself stretched out on the tarmac of a Liverpool car park, trouserless. He couldn't remember how he'd got there, who he'd been with, or why. Barney panicked; and the morning rush hour was enlivened by the unusual sight of a lanky John Cleese figure silly-walking down Lime Street with his shirt tails flapping above his long, bony legs, accusing innocent passers-by of having nicked Old Barney's kecks.*

*Barney always blamed the idiosyncrasies of London Transport for his habit of either turning up at gigs that weren't booked or not turning up at gigs that were. Grudgingly awarding him the benefit of the doubt, Ken forked out for a Vespa motor scooter to enable Barney to get around. For a week all went well; Barney chugged along to each gig on his scooter just on the right side of opening time, and then chugged off home again*

47

*after the session was over.*

*Then one night he turned up at a gig an hour late and Vespa-less. He claimed he'd parked his scooter that afternoon on some quiet London street, the name of which he'd forgotten, and had spent the rest of the day searching for it. Not long after the disappearance of his Vespa, Barney disappeared too. The Vespa was never recovered, but Barney did eventually reappear on the gig circuit working for the Acker Bilk and, later, Terry Lightfoot bands.*

*Barney's replacement, Ron 'Weathers' Weatherburn, was a weird character. He was way ahead of his time - from a negative standpoint, that is. In the days when Mick Jagger would still have been sporting a staid short-back-and-sides, Weathers often wore his hair shoulder-length. He also foreshadowed the destructive tendencies of groups like The Who, once pushing an upright piano off a high stage because it was out of tune (it certainly was after that!) and on another occasion throwing a TV set out of a second-floor hotel room window, claiming it was too noisy. In his quieter moments Ron would rapidly polish off the Times Ximenes crossword and he was among only a handful of Times crossword solvers ever to win the prize of a Chambers dictionary twice.*

*Ron was a whizz-kid on ragtime piano. Audiences adored him, particularly when he embarked on one of his showpiece solo numbers, such as Jelly Roll Morton's 'Fingerbuster', on which he sounded like three piano rolls being played simultaneously. During these solos he sat with legs entwined round his piano stool, arms flailing over the keyboard, yet still finding time to pick his nose with his left forefinger (his right forefinger being reserved for rubbing his eye through the one vacant lens in his spectacles, which had been crushed during some long-forgotten fracas). At the end of one of these recitals he would rudely snub the applause from his army of fans by giving them an insolent V-sign and a sardonic smile. Weathers usually got away with his rebel-without-a-cause act: jazz audiences loved it; women mothered him; men humoured him.*

*Ron Weatherburn didn't suffer fools gladly, and his wit could be*

48

*corrosive. At one jazz jamboree, at a well-known seaside resort, all the musicians from every band on the bill were invited to a reception attended by the local dignitaries. We were formed into a long, straggly row to meet the mayor, who then proceeded grandly down the line, making inane comments to each musician along the way. After being introduced to Weathers the mayor asked him which band he played for. Ron gave his warning lop-sided smile. "Ball's!" he blurted. Conversation ebbed; heads turned. The mayor, unsure whether or not he'd been insulted, looked flustered. Ron stared him out, while the mayor grew redder in the face, and then reached forward and tugged at the mayor's chain of office. "I've got one like this in my bog at home," he confided. "Mine flushes, too."*

# 5
# ON THE ROAD

*John:*

*Back in the days of the 'Trad Boom' there were a lot of them about. Many's the time I've stood at a draughty roadside, waiting for one that was overdue, only to see three go by at once, headed for anywhere between Land's End and John o' Groats. They came in all shapes, colours and states of mechanical health, and they were regarded by their passengers as necessary conveniences (often in more ways than one). They were band buses.*

*These days, band bus spotting has lost its edge. Not only are there considerably fewer band buses to spot, but also those that are still around are hardly worth a second glance. The glorious psychedelic charabancs of yesteryear, whose accommodation was sometimes reduced to one infested mattress in the shadowed area behind the driver's seat, have since been replaced by more upmarket versions with reclining seats, windows, heaters and interior lights.*

*Kenny:*

We purchased our first bandwagon, a Bedford Dormobile, from an animal rescue organisation. I had to hose it down, wash it out and put some seats in the back. I went to a breaker's yard and bought the front bench seat off an American car, which would seat three people. It was only a pound. Then I noticed all these brown stains on it. So before I screwed it onto the Dormobile I gave it a good wash, only to find that all those brown stains turned bright red - it was blood! I just hosed it all down and then bolted it in. I've never told anybody about this before. All those people who sat in it were actually sitting where somebody had had a terrible accident. But there you go.

**John:**

*I didn't know that - it's the first I've heard about it. And you kept it quiet for 50 years!*

*Like most jazz musicians, I have a love-hate relationship with tour buses in general. This is because musicians and their bandwagons spend as much time together as an old married couple, and even the most up-to-date and sexiest vehicle can have its wrong time of the month. On the other hand, the band bus offers a temporary safe haven. Inside there's always enough space to lounge, read, nosh and do all kinds of other things, depending on one's aspirations and the current state of play. In fact, the relationship of a jazz musician to his bus resembles that of a sailor to his ship. All of us at one time or another have made the late dash for our set of wheels, and have leapt on board with a sigh of relief moments before it would've weighed anchor, so to speak, and sailed out of harbour without us.*

*Having in my time travelled many thousands of miles in a wide variety of these horseless carriages, I ought to feel a twinge of nostalgia for at least one or two of them. Oddly enough, I don't. Looking back over the cavalcade of eccentric vehicles we've driven into the ground over the past five decades, all that springs to mind is a catalogue of misfortunes, frustrations and disasters.*

*Take our very first bandwagon, the aforementioned Bedford Dormobile, a temperamental van without windows or proper seats (and, as is now apparent, a darker history than most of us realised!) One night, back in the late 1950s, we were rounding Trafalgar Square after midnight when drummer Ron Bowden, who was driving, spotted something rather unusual. A wheel was rolling smoothly past us on the inside lane. Some joker pointed out that, as we were doing a legal 30mph, the wheel must've been speeding. Our chuckles died away, however, when we realised that it was actually our own rear wheel that was overtaking us! We ground to a halt. A policeman rapped on Ron's window, so Ron tried to open the sliding door. Instead of sliding, however, it fell straight out onto the policeman's feet! I don't know how we got away with that.*

**Kenny:**

After the Dormobile we had a Volkswagen van. Ron Bowden was driving that one, too, when it rolled over a couple of times on an icy road outside Dundee. We were all, Ron included, well pissed, having just left a raving party at the university. When the thing came to a standstill we all got out and rolled the van upright. That's when we heard a little voice saying, "Can somebody please help me?" It turned out to be our banjo player of the time, Bill Dixon. He'd been sitting in the back with all the gear and we'd forgotten all about him! But after we'd pulled him out of the rubble of drums and amplifiers he was as good as new. That Volkswagen, with its crumpled roof, cracked windows and doors tied together with string got us through the remainder of that Scottish tour. Those old VW vans were mighty hardy vehicles, I can tell you!

**John:**

*On that occasion I remember waking up to find my seat on the 'ceiling' above my head. All the passengers had done a complete somersault without realising it and we'd all resumed our usual seated formation in an upside-down bus!*

**Kenny:**

The Commer bus came after the Volkswagen in 1962. As we were getting rich (!) we decided to buy a brand new, top-of-the-range van and get it fitted out. Trouble was, I bought a straight van, and being completely stupid I didn't take into account that it had van springing, which was pretty hard. Anyhow, at first we thought it was wonderful. The seats were like deckchairs, with tubular steel frames bolted to the floor - this is what luxury was like for us in those days. The seats were a kind of padded, leather-like material, which we reclined on. However, they became bloody uncomfortable after the first couple of hundred miles. And the springing! Every time we went over a bump all the seats jerked flat and we ended up on the floor. There's an article about it in Motor Transport. Our top-of-the-range motor!

### John:

*It was big and rust-red. It boasted the very latest in state-of-the-art bandwagon technology, with seats specially designed for us by Barking Garage, who claimed to know all about these things. Those seats were revolutionary in every sense. You could turn them back to front if you wanted to, but no one ever did. Instead, we spent much of each journey lying in involuntary reclining positions on the deck after hitting the slightest bit of unevenness in the road.*

### Kenny:

Once, back in the early '60s, thieves broke into our bandwagon while it was parked overnight. Everything was taken. But then the police told us they'd received a phone call from an old lady who was getting a bit agitated over a large object that looked to have been planted overnight at the bottom of her garden. I think she thought it might have something to do with a UFO. It turned out to be Vic Pitt's bass, which the thieves must've decided was of no use to them, because they'd thrown it over her wall. It had landed upright in her flower bed, the spike planting it among her lupins.

So Vic had got his bass back and was the luckiest of us all - for a while. A few weeks later Vic Pitt's bass was involved in another bandwagon incident, this time on the M1, which had then only recently been opened. We were all looking out the back windows of the van when the bass slid off the roof rack over our heads. We saw it hit the motorway, and a split-second later an artic ran over it and turned it into matchwood!

### John:

*I've noticed, over the years, a weird kind of symmetry in incidents involving our various bandwagons. For instance, on one occasion, back in the early 1960s, we'd all been reclining comfortably in our parked-up Volkswagen minibus when it ran forwards across a road in Denmark and smacked into a high brick wall. This was echoed in the early 1970s, when our Mercedes van slid **backwards** down a slope in Scotland, where it ended up perched on the top of a low brick wall. We piled out of one wagon in double-quick time, when it suddenly caught fire on the A1; we piled into another just as quickly in Stirling, and drove off at speed when a group of Scottish football fans started throwing beer bottles at us just because their team lost. Defunct vehicles of ours have been pulled out of muddy fields by farm tractors or, in one instance, pushed by a car several miles across Scandinavia in a forlorn attempt to catch an overnight ferry. A Ford Transit was written off completely after skidding head-on into a tree; another became similarly incapacitated after hitting a cow. The list goes on.*

### Kenny:

One morning we parked our van in a busy street in Liverpool while we went for a Chinese meal. We knew about the reputation of that part of Liverpool, so we took it in turns to go out every few minutes to check whether the bandwagon was still there. It was, but when we got into it we found the inside had been completely ransacked. How that had been done, we've no idea, but for their ingenuity we had to hand it to the pilferers - and, of course, we did, literally.

**John:**

*I wouldn't say any of us have been really envious of another band's vehicle, but I do confess to having a sneaking regard for Acker Bilk's dark green Mercedes van, which, although now long defunct, seemed during the 1980s to have been around almost as long as he has. Nicknamed the Green Goddess, with its rakish lines, dark green paintwork and large spare tank slung under the chassis, it had the swashbuckling appearance of an RAF Lancaster equipped for dambusting.*

*Some of the more imaginative souls in our profession have, in fact, noticed the superficial resemblance between setting out on a long overnight trip back to London in a dodgy vehicle in winter and preparing for take-off in the 'Memphis Belle' on its umpteenth mission over enemy territory. Here we come, trooping in line out of the stage door of the municipal hall, muffled up to the eyebrows in windcheaters and leatherware, hauling ourselves one by one aboard our bus, clambering over luggage with the sure-footedness of mountain goats into our appointed positions (which some of us have occupied for decades). The engine roars doubtfully into life; someone pores over a map with a torch - bomb aimer to navigator - and it's chocks away, lads!*

**Kenny:**

My first roadie was Bill Bowyer, and he was my cousin. He was a funny bloke; full of beans and tram tickets, as they say. Unfortunately, Bill had a couple of drinks one night and got pulled up coming back from a German drinking club in Bristol. He was breathalysed and banned from driving, so I had to put him in the office as manager. He hated it. Eventually, he got fed up with going up to London and sitting in the office all day and left. But he used to come up with some wonderful sayings. He'd stand by the side of the stage doing the amplification, saying, "Come on, lads, give it crutch" - meaning, put some bollocks into it! He loved the band. And he could imitate Lonnie

Donegan very well. He used to hold a tennis racket as his 'banjo' and he knew all Lonnie's songs.

There was one instance when we made a single - it wasn't one of our hit records; in fact it went down like a lead balloon. It was called 'Morocco '64'. At that time I think all the songwriters and composers were worried about their car payments and were trying to get one enormous hit record out of us. Anyway, somebody put us onto this tune, which I think was the theme tune from a TV drama series.

While we were making the record Bill Bowyer, who was in the studio, was yelling, "Come on lads, give it crutch," and so on. It got a bit annoying, so to give him something to keep him occupied we let him crash a cymbal at the very end of the number. We thought, well, all Moroccan music had cymbals, didn't it - or anywhere east of France, come to that? "Hit the cymbal," I told him, "and then keep quiet for a few seconds until the tape stops." We got a perfect take for 'Morocco '64' - not a very good record, I must be honest! - but the actual recording was flawless: a rare thing for us. At that time recording generally was a bit uncivilised and pretty hard to get right. Anyhow, Bill got to the end, and BANG! "How's that, Ken?" he yelled. We didn't know until we heard the playback that Bill's shout had ruined the take and we'd have to do it all again.

One rainy afternoon in a city up north - it might've been Leeds - Bill and I were looking out of the lounge window of our digs, and I said, "I've written a melody, Bill. Fancy helping me write the words?" He said he'd love to. So we composed this song called 'Harmonise' and Bill wrote some of the words. Some time later I took it to the recording studio, where we were making a record along with Max Bygraves. I showed it to Max and he said he'd think about recording it. So, to encourage him to record the song, we offered him half the royalties. That meant that Bill and I would get a quarter each and Max

Bygraves would get half. Anyway, Max recorded it with us. Then some months later I saw Max at a concert. He didn't know I was in the audience, and he announced, "I'd like to sing a song that I wrote myself. It's called 'Harmonise'." And he proceeded to sing 'Harmonise' exactly the way Bill and I had written it. I thought, bloody hell ...! But there you are; it's just one of those things. And I've never had any royalties for it since.

After Bill left us we had another roadie who's now become the mayor of St Ives, Cornwall. In the early '60s he'd regularly turn up at our gigs with a tin of Harpic lavatory cleaner, which he'd leave on the front of the stage. He'd say, "All right, Ken?" and off he'd go, jiving away in his strange clobber. Once I asked him what the Harpic tin was for, and he replied, "I'm clean round the bend!"

### John:

*He dressed in what looked like a kind of monk's habit and was known to all as Harry Harpic, because he hung this battered, empty Harpic tin from a pyjama cord strung round his waist. As his fame grew, Harry needed only to enter a jazz club, raise the tin on high and exclaim "Harpic!" to arouse a whole army of followers, who would then chant in unison, "GOES CLEAN ROUND THE BEND!" Harry had that effect on people. He was a Pied Piper of jazz. Once he led about 150 of the great unwashed across Europe just for them all to exclaim, "GOES CLEAN ROUND THE BEND!" to an audience of 2,000 puzzled French citizens during our concert at a jazz festival in Antibes back in July 1961. I think it was his offbeat notoriety that encouraged Ken to sign him up as a roadie.*

### Kenny:

By the way, at that jazz festival in Antibes we were on the same bill as Ray Charles. It was funny. When we played our last tune, 'Muskrat Ramble', they announced us off to roars of applause, and then on shuffled Ray Charles with a group of terrifically good black musicians. So, of course, there was the grand announcement, "Ladies and Gentlemen, the one and only Mr Ray Charles," and they started Count Basie's 'Lil' Darling' at an unbelievably slow tempo. We'd never heard it played as slow as that before and we couldn't believe it. There's a recorded version of it around somewhere. Anyhow, it was a terrific band, as I said, and the Raelets were there with him, too. (I love the joke: "How do you become a Raelet?" "All you have to do is let Ray." There was some truth in that, too.)

At Antibes, Beryl Bryden - 'Britain's Queen of the Blues' - was on the bill. And, of course, she was a very big lady. Anyhow, we were all sitting on the beach and the tide takes a little while to go out there. It's kind of a shallow seabed, so you can walk out into the water and after 50 yards or so you're still able to stand. While we were sitting there, all of a sudden we spotted what looked like a seal or a walrus in the distance. As it got closer to the shore, it suddenly stood up - and it was Beryl. She was wearing a one-piece silver swimming costume and had been swimming on her back - you can imagine.

Anyway, all that was before I asked Harry Harpic to join the band. But he was with us in 1964, when we went on a cruise on the SS *Arcadia*. He used to drink in the engineers' quarters in the deck below our first-class one. All booze on ships is about half to a quarter of the normal price, and it cost virtually nothing in the engineers' quarters. Harry went down there regularly. One time he got sick through drinking too much and he went to the toilet and lost his false teeth down the plughole (clean round the bend!) He thought he could get them back, but by then they were already at the bottom of the Mediterranean. Because Harry didn't come back up to our deck, someone thought he must've fallen overboard and reported him missing. The ship had to do a U-turn in search of him. When he did finally turn up there was a terrible fuss. For a start, he shouldn't have strayed down to the lower decks, and the captain was not too pleased that he'd had to go on a fruitless search.

## John:

*Harry's record still stands as the only roadie that managed to drive our Volkswagen van by remote control. He'd stopped at a garage to buy himself a packet of fags, but had left the handbrake off when he got out. The van, with the rest of us inside, was parked on a slope and slowly moved out of the entrance, cruised down the hill and finally came to a standstill in someone's driveway. Harry wasn't at all fazed by his mistake. "Couldn't you lot wait just five minutes," he huffed irritably when he finally caught us up.*

## Kenny:

Some 40 years ago, on one of our world tours, we worked in a big casino club on the outskirts of Sydney known locally as the Taj Mahal - because of its architecture, I suppose. After a month there we went on to Melbourne for a week or two, playing in a hotel. Our roadie at the time was a huge fellow - wide rather than tall, if you know what I mean. His name was Mick Jones. He'd met a bird in Sydney, an Australian girl, whom he thought he'd fallen in love with. Anyhow, when we went to Melbourne she came along and they shacked up in a hotel room and virtually disappeared while we were there. At the end of the fortnight we were due to leave for England. Mick came to me and said, "I'm not going back. I'm going off with my girlfriend." He'd borrowed loads of money off the blokes in the band, and just as we were leaving he gave me a hotel bill for £900, which you can imagine 40 years ago was a lot of money. But I had to pay it, otherwise they wouldn't let us out. And Mick Jones stayed behind, with no money to get back. The promoter was very kind and left Mick's return ticket at his agent's office in Melbourne.

So off we went, and off he went with his girlfriend up into the mountains or somewhere. He owed the boys money, he'd sold someone's record player, and his £900 bill was mostly for stuff like champagne. I can still see it all now. Mick Jones had phoned his wife and two kids on his birthday to tell her he wasn't coming home! Meanwhile, I'd phoned my wife just to tell her that Mick was staying in Australia. She was friends with Mick's wife, who lived in Luton, so she immediately phoned her to get the full story. Then my wife phoned me. And I'll tell you something: I didn't need a telephone to hear her, even though she was 12,000 miles away! Anyhow, we eventually got back, and my wife came to understand that people do sometimes do silly things like that.

About six months later I got a telephone call from Mick Jones to ask me for a reference -he'd got a job working at Vauxhall's in Luton as a security officer! I said I couldn't give him a reference after all his antics. And, believe it or not, he was upset about that - and this was someone who'd stolen about £1,000 (about £5,000 today, I suppose)! That was the last I heard of him. I think he did go back to his wife and two kids (and I'm sure they always sing 'Happy Birthday' on his birthday!)

He was a bit lairy - and I was a bit naïve. When he was first with the band he told me he'd seen an American car for sale: a big five-seater. "We could all travel in that," he said. "And it's only 500 quid." And I believed him. I paid him the 500 quid and away we went up to Scotland. God knows how we got there. The bloody thing coughed and spluttered constantly, and it very soon ended up on the scrap heap. It was an absolutely awful car; it was a wreck. It turned out he'd bought it for £100 and charged me £500. How the naïve live!

I had another roadie from North London who insisted on parking our minibus outside his house. He picked up a few parking fines because of that. Eventually he ended up with £300 of them - this must be 20 years ago - and the law said if you don't pay up you're going to jail. Well, I decided I'd have to pay them and take it out of his wages, as I was perfectly willing to pay for him to garage it somewhere. Anyhow, they got him to court and gave him three months in jail. He phoned me from the court, saying he'd be leaving within the hour to do three months in Pentonville. I was living in Hornchurch at the time. So I got some cash and shot over to the court. I got there just as the prison van, with all the prisoners inside, was exiting - it was actually on the move. I pulled up in front of it, got out and shouted, "Stop! Stop! Stop!" They halted the vehicle and I asked them to let my bloke out, explaining that I would pay the £300 in cash to stop him from going to jail. They were very kind. At that time I suppose I was recognised - a 'celebrity'. Anyway, I took him in to see the clerk of the court, paid the 300 quid, and the clerk thanked me very much and shook my hand. So that roadie didn't go to jail - but it was the last I saw of him.

There was another roadie that lived in Peterborough and it cost an awful lot of money in diesel going backwards and forwards from there. One time I found a bill he'd given me from the petrol company that showed he'd bought a shell suit for about £50. On my bill! So I complained about it. I said, "Why throw money away? You don't need a shell suit," to which he replied, "Oh, I do. It's for - you know - filling up with diesel and all that." Eventually I had to get rid of him, because he was not very good at the sound and he was lazy. So he took me to court and demanded £11,000 compensation for unfair dismissal! I told him to stick it where the sun don't shine. We had our day in court and they told him to piss off (in legal terms). So he did. And that was the last I saw of him.

**John:**

*I remember one incident involving that roadie (who, for want of a better name, I shall call Pete). It happened in a restaurant in Germany. Pete,* who was a bit of a show-off at the best of times, was eager to demonstrate to everyone his command of the German language. So, in a very loud voice, he called out for his restaurant bill. A hush descended in the restaurant. Heads turned and people regarded Pete coldly. The blushing waitress glared at him, smacked the table with the palm of her hand and flounced off. What had Pete said that was so terrible? It transpired that Pete had made a small error in his pronunciation. What should've been *"Bezahlen Bitte!"* had been misinterpreted as *"Besamen Bitte!"* which, as every German knows (but we didn't until we were told,) translates as, *"Please accept a specimen of my sperm!"*

# 6
# THE HIT YEARS

*Kenny:*

By 1960 we were making headlines. And the man in charge at our very first audition in a London studio - for a television spot with ITV that we'd applied for - was the director of the London Palladium. That was around April 1960, as I recall. The audition was at Cecil Sharpe House and I think three people were there, including the producer, of course, and his secretary. Anyhow, we were doing the audition in front of him, and at the same time Lonnie Donegan was rehearsing nearby and he overheard us. By that time Lonnie was a huge star and was presenting his own ITV show, Putting on the Donegan (named after his biggest hit, 'Putting on the Style'). We were playing 'South Rampart Street Parade', I think.

In Lonnie came and - after he'd chatted to his old mate, our drummer Ron Bowden, whom he'd known during his days with the Chris Barber band - he turned and said, "Who are you?"

"Kenny Ball," I replied.

"Well, the band sounds really good," said Lonnie. "What are you doing here?"

"We're auditioning for a television show."

"Do you want a television show?" he asked.

"Yes," I replied.

"Then you've got one," came the response. "You can come on Putting on the Donegan." Then he continued, "And have you got a recording contract?"

"No," said I.

"You've got one now," he said, just like that.

At that point I discovered that Lonnie was also an A&R man for Pye Records. So all of our dreams - as well as Steve Race's - came true in that one afternoon. In May that year we started recording for Pye, and on 14 July 1960 we appeared on Lonnie's TV show.

### John:

*A&R stands for Artists and Repertoire. A&R men are responsible for talent scouting and overseeing the artistic output of recording artists. They're expected to understand the current tastes of the market and to be able to find artists that will be commercially successful. This is why A&R people are often former musicians, like Lonnie Donegan, or record producers, like Alan A. Freeman (no relation to the famous, late, disc jockey nicknamed 'Fluff'). Lonnie had helped us on our first recording, but even then Alan A. Freeman was always in the background. He was The Man.*

### Kenny:

Alan Freeman was probably the greatest A&R man that ever existed. He did all Petula Clark's stuff, all Lonnie Donegan's stuff and then settled on us! We were so lucky to have him. He was such a devoted fan of the band; a lovely man. He got on with the band like a house on fire.

Our first single was 'Teddy Bear's Picnic'. Lonnie picked that one, you see, because he thought we were like another Chris Barber band - which we weren't really. But you have to remember we were young; full of beans and tram tickets. I was in my mid-twenties and John Bennett was a bit younger. At least two or three nights a week we'd be playing in jazz clubs. They were always the same ones and they always had the same people in the audience, too. You'd go back there every month, so you really had to find new tunes to play. And the tunes that appealed to us were those with good chordal and melodic sequences. Once you've played 'When the Saints Go Marching In' 3,000 times you have a tendency to think, well what can I find to play on it now? It's possible to replicate the thing, of course, and still love the idiom, but by playing something new on a new tune you get something new back. And that was our idea.

Our band was terrific and full of life. That was probably why we got on so well with Lonnie, because both of us don't take no prisoners when we perform. Lonnie was a great banjo player who swung like the clappers and did till the day he died. One night when we were due to play in the 100 Club in London's Oxford Street in the early '60s my banjo player fell sick, so I phoned Lonnie and asked him if he could come and join us. "How much is it worth?" he asked. I said, "A fiver." "Done," came the reply. And at that time Lonnie would've been going out for around £200 a night!

How did we make up the arrangements on things like 'Teddy Bear's Picnic'? Well, I would play the lead, John would find another harmony and, of course, Dave Jones, with his fantastic harmonic sense, would find the third part. In fact, sometimes I'd play the same phrase over a different chord and instantly Dave could alter his harmony to fit it perfectly. He'd have the harmony ready before I'd even played the phrase.

### John:

*At that time I don't think any of us really expected the Kenny Ball Band to crack the hit parade. In those days trad jazz bands that had already had hit records - like Chris Barber with 'Petite Fleur' and Acker Bilk with 'Summerset' and later on 'Stranger on the Shore' - were criticised in some quarters as having 'gone commercial'. Bands who 'played to the masses' were a severe disappointment to the purists. At that time we didn't think of ourselves as commercial in that sense. But, as we were shortly to find out, the word "Commercial!" sounds very much like an expletive when spat in your face by an irate jazz enthusiast!*

*In the meantime, 'Teddy Bears', along with the rest of the titles we'd recorded, were released on the first Kenny Ball album, Invitation to the Ball. The recording sessions had been undertaken in our spare time, i.e., in the dead of night when all decent people are fast asleep. They were fairly riotous occasions for one and all, including teetotal Lonnie, who took over the banjo playing during 'Dinah', leaving Diz Disley with two free hands with which to make rude gestures while singing the vocal. Unlike singles, albums never got tagged as commercial, and this one received good reviews in the music press - particularly from our mentor, Steve Race, who also contributed the programme notes.*

*Sometime during the autumn of 1960 Kenny was interviewed by Brian Nicholls, columnist for the magazine Jazz News. Brian reminded Kenny that his band was now generally reckoned as number three, just below Chris Barber's and Acker Bilk's.*

*"What next, Kenny?" he asked. "How are you going to make the jump into their part of the entertainment business?"*

*"Wish I knew, Dad," Kenny had replied. "It's too easy to slip into a safe routine."*

*In his article Nicholls concluded, "Kenny has a drive that makes him want something bigger and better all the time. And making money is a real target. There is more of the business man in Kenny Ball than in most jazz musicians."*

### Kenny:

Well, by this time we were going strong. We were breaking attendance records all over the country and had broadcast on BBC Radio 2's *Saturday Club* for Brian Matthew - our great friend and supporter - for the first time in July 1960. But it was really *Easy Beat* - a fantastic show on the 'BBC Light Programme', also presented by Brian - that really launched the band into the limelight. *Easy Beat* was pre-recorded on Wednesday nights in front of a huge audience at the famous 'home of light entertainment': the Palace Theatre in Lower Regent Street. It was then put out at 10.30 on Sunday mornings, and it was huge for us. We appeared on the show for the first time in September 1960 and later played on it every week until June 1961, which was probably some kind of a record, I think. It must've been - at least until The Beatles came along.

### John:

*Our most memorable session on* Easy Beat *came shortly after New Year's Day 1961. The band played its usual quota of six numbers, and one tune in particular really raised the roof. The studio audience - all rock 'n' roll fans - gave it such an ovation that when the recording was trimmed for transmission almost a minute's applause had to be cut from the tape. When the show was broadcast that following Sunday morning it became clear that the majority of* Easy Beat's *6.5 million radio listeners were every bit as excited by the Kenny Ball Band's 'new' sound as the studio audience. From then on, every gig we played was packed out. Very soon afterwards the band was given an extended contract to appear on* Easy Beat *every week.*

*In his book,* Trad Mad, *Brian Matthew explains how the Kenny Ball Band came to be invited onto his* Easy Beat *show in the first place. "Towards the end of 1960," he writes, "... I was a producer with a headache ... Quite suddenly the show needed a shot in the arm." Jim Davidson, then assistant head of Light Entertainment for the BBC, demanded a new ingredient. Brian, who had recently featured the Kenny Ball Band on one of his* Saturday Club *broadcasts, suggested that the band should be given a spot on* Easy Beat *too. Jim Davidson wasn't convinced;* Saturday Club *featured middle-of-the-road music, he said, and traditional jazz just about fell into that category, but it was unlikely to appeal to* Easy Beat's *youthful pop audience. Even so, he grudgingly allowed the experiment to go ahead 'with appropriate caution' during the first four weeks of 1961.*

*"Well all that is ancient history," writes Brian. "The band made a colossal impact on its very first show, our audience increased by leaps and bounds, and Kenny's contract was increased until he eventually stayed on the show for seven months without a break."*

*The number on that first* Easy Beat *show that had raised such a commotion among jazz and pop fans alike was 'Samantha', a vocal by Kenny that had been introduced into the band's repertoire almost by accident.*

### Kenny:

Why did we go for 'Samantha'? Well, we were playing at a club called the Iron Door - in Liverpool again - and there was a bloke called Cyril there who was a bit of a piano player. We were having a bit of a late-night jam session, you see, while packing up our gear after the gig was over, and he sat at the piano and said, "You ought to play this song - and record it." And he played 'Samantha'. We looked at each other and said, "Yes, that sounds nice." I think what attracted us really was the chord sequence and also the fast tempo, because everyone knew it as a slow song, of course. Bing and Louis had sung it in *High Society*, but as a slow ballad. We speeded it up and gave it that eight-to-the-bar shuffle, which was great for the dancers, too. And Lonnie liked it, so he made it our single of the moment - though at the time I was quite keen on 'Seventy-six Trombones' from *The Music Man*. But Lonnie won the argument – and, of course, he was right.

Anyhow, after another short trip to Germany we got back and found 'Samantha' in the charts. The *Juke Box Jury* panel voted it a hit and only old Arthur Askey gave it the thumbs down: "I'm not a jazz fan," he said. That was in February 1961, and on 4 March 1961 'Samantha' entered the *New Musical Express* charts at number 17 and stayed in the Top 20 for the next 15 weeks.

Naturally, when you've got a hit record that's just about the biggest thing that can happen. Our money went up, too. The year before, we would've got around £15-£20 for the whole band, but now we were getting £100-£120 a night, which was a lot of money back then.

When 'Samantha' went into the charts I had to see that producer again at his office in Regent Street, because now he wanted us to play at the London Palladium.

"Ah, Mr Baker," he said.

"Yes."

"I've just been listening to your record Sumatra ..."

That bodes well, I thought.

But anyhow, there we were in the charts - and the top band of the year - and the only way to go seemed to be up.

Then, of course, there was Clinton Ford. We first met Clinton at an after-hours drink-up at the Press Club in Liverpool. He had a tremendous stage presence. Most of the night he would be sitting on a stool in the centre of that club with his guitar, and he'd just kind of hold everyone's attention, singing his songs and mixing it with humour. Not long after we first met him he came down from Liverpool to join my band on our Easy Beat broadcasts.

Well, he was a great singer, but he suffered from the most awful nerves and sometimes couldn't go onto the stage. So by 1962 he'd decided instead to go freelance and work with Diz Disley's band, The Bards. Later he went to live on the Isle of Man, where he opened a boarding house. He never really came back, though I know he sang with Liverpool's Merseysippi Band later on. He broke up with his wife and he had terrible troubles with allergies, too - he could only eat lettuce and a bit of cheese or whatever. Sadly, Clinton died in 2009.

*John:*
*Our follow-up to 'Samantha' was 'I Still Love You All'. "Six months*

ago," wrote a Disc journalist, "it probably would not even have been reviewed on this page." He meant that as a compliment. Kenny Ball's 'Samantha', he wrote, had "achieved what used to be a near impossible feat for his kind of music - a position in the never-never land of the Best Sellers. If you don't react to this side, man you is dead!"

The New Musical Express on 12 May announced that 'I Still Love You All' had "flashed into the NME chart at No. 18 to join the still popular 'Samantha' (now No. 25)." The writer had dropped in on Kenny at the London Palladium to find him still dazed at the band's current success. The NME article concluded: "'It's amazing', Kenny exclaimed, running his hand through his sleek black hair. 'Do you know, people on the Tube nudge each other now and whisper "That's Kenny Ball!" I can't get over it'."

*Melody Maker, 13 May 1961:*
*Busy 24 hours in the life of Kenny Ball*

**KENNY BALL's JAZZMEN had the busiest 24 hours of their lives last weekend.**
**On Friday night they started work on their new album for Pye Records, finishing at 4 a.m.**
**At 11 a.m. on Saturday they were at Wood Green to rehearse a spot in ATV's "All Kinds Of Music" - at the same time as they were on the air in the Light Programme's pre-recorded "Saturday Club."**
**At 2.15 p.m. they were at the London Palladium for a matinee performance.**
**They had a second Palladium show, ending their spot at 7.14 p.m., and left by car for Wood Green to film "All Kinds Of Music."**
**At 9.08.p.m. they were back on stage at the Palladium.**

*And so to bed*

*At 10.30 p.m. they left for Pye Studios to complete the recording session. This ended at 4.30 a.m. when a very tired band headed for bed.*

*The band ends its two weeks at the London Palladium tomorrow (Saturday), and on Sunday has two sessions - at Southend Pier in the afternoon and Jazzshows Jazz Club in the evening.*

### John:

*The band's third single was an old jazz standard: 'Someday You'll Be Sorry', a song composed by Louis Armstrong. On the B-side was a Kenny original: 'Lumbered at the Lotus'. Its title referred to his favourite Chinese restaurant, the Lotus House in the Edgware Road, close to Pye Studios at Marble Arch, in which on one notorious occasion our leader had been duly 'lumbered' by having to pick up the tab for the entire party!*

*Soon afterwards 'Someday You'll Be Sorry' moved into the hit parade and stayed there for six weeks. The Kenny Ball Band could now boast three successive hits, all of which had been vocals. Our recording manager, Alan A. Freeman, suggested that it was time to change the formula - our next single should be an instrumental.*

### Kenny:

Originally 'Moscow' was brought to us by one of the record company representatives. It was on a demo disc by a Dutch band, but nothing like our version - we completely changed it. And I think the reason why we changed it was the tempo, because at that time when we were playing everyone in the audience got up and danced. And I remember Bonnie Manzi, the owner of the Brighton jazz club, saying, "Kenny, my boy, if you get them up dancing, you've got a successful band!" So we decided to play the tune with a sort of two-beat feel; not too fast!

**John:**

At rehearsal our cup mutes didn't have quite the sound that Ken was looking for, so we experimented with various vessels we found lying around in the studio: pint mugs, ashtrays, even fire buckets. None sounded right. During the lunch break Ken scoured the hardware shops looking for a different kind of mute. He returned with a pair of children's potties - a pink one for himself and a blue one for me. Held over the bells of our instruments they produced exactly the melancholy hollow sound we wanted.

Ken was so pleased with his pink potty that after recording 'Midnight in Moscow' he would use nothing else - for a mute, that is! The original receptacle, featured in many a stage and TV appearance in the years to come, became something of a conversation piece among audiences the world over. Naturally, over the years it took quite a beating, and that legendary jazz artefact - travel-weary, battered, scarred with cigarette burns and held together with gaffer tape - is now, alas, no more. Ken now uses a potty that looks so like the original, including the cigarette burns, that he might've actually commissioned it with 'Midnight in Moscow' in mind! Ken claims the present potty once belonged to his son, Keith - though, fortunately, as far as we know Keith hasn't used it for 50 years!

The record was released in November 1961. In the same week the band performed along with Acker Bilk and the Temperance Seven in that year's Royal Variety Show, attended by the Queen Mother. 'TRAD STRIKES ERMINSVILLE!' blared **Melody Maker**'s headline. It was a good omen: just a few days later 'Midnight in Moscow' entered the charts at lucky number 13.

When Pye Records' press office phoned the Russian Embassy for information about the tune they were informed that Russia didn't have a Top Ten - though if it had, added their informant, it would certainly be its number one, as 'Midnight in Moscow' was Khrushchev's favourite song. Encouraged by that, the Pye press agent sent one copy of 'Midnight in Moscow' to the Russian Embassy in London and another direct to

*Nikita Khrushchev at the Kremlin. Neither was acknowledged.*

*Herbert Kretzmer, songwriter and critic, stated in a* **Daily Express** *article that the composers of the song, comrades V. Soloviev and M. Matusovsky, would not be receiving a penny in royalties from our record. This, added Mr Kretzmer, was only right and proper since the Russians had never paid royalties to the West for anything and therefore should expect none in return. By that time 'Midnight in Moscow' had reached number four in the British hit parade and was also a hit in India, Italy, Japan, Norway, Sweden, Denmark and Eire. In early 1962 the record peaked at number two on the US Billboard Hot 100 chart, and in March of that year it spent three weeks at number one on the American Easy Listening chart.*

*A current American website, The Big Bands Database, states: "Following their first big hit 'Samantha', the Kenny Ball band would go on to score hit after hit, including fourteen top thirty records - an achievement which has never been equalled by any other Jazz artist. Interestingly, this eclipsed even Kenny's idol, the great Louis Armstrong's total."*

*Almost unbelievably, the band had now reached the front line of the pop scene, and during this period Pye Records were releasing a new Kenny Ball single every three months. Even less believably, Ken was informed that his latest single, 'March of the Siamese Children', had reached number one in the* **New Musical Express** *charts! Actually, people can be forgiven for thinking that the Kenny Ball Band never had a number one, as the record stayed at that position for just two weeks. And since then the* **Guinness Book of Records** *has consistently ignored the fact, placing the highest position of 'Siamese' at number four in its charts. However, among my collection of ephemera I do have the evidence (see over):*

*Compiled from dealers' returns from all over Britain.*

## Week ending March 10th, 1962

| Last Week | This Week | Title | Artist | Label |
|---|---|---|---|---|
| 1 | 1 | March Of The Siamese Children - - - | Kenny Ball | Pye |
| 2 | 2 | Rock-A-Hula Baby/Can't Help Falling In Love - - - - - - - - - | Elvis Presley | RCA |
| 6 | 3 | Wonderful Land - - - - - - - - | The Shadows | Columbia |
| 5 | 4 | Tell Me What He Said - - - - - - | Helen Shapiro | Columbia |
| 4 | 5 | The Young Ones - - - - - - - | Cliff Richard | Columbia |
| 3 | 6 | Wimoweh - - - - - - - - | Karl Denver | Decca |
| 7 | 7 | Let's Twist Again - - - - - - | Chubby Checker | Columbia |
| 10 | 8 | Crying In The Rain - - - - - - | Everly Brothers | Warner Bros |
| 9 | 9 | Walk On By - - - - - - - | Leroy Van Dyke | Mercury |
| 11 | 10 | Stranger On The Shore - - - - - | Acker Bilk | Columbia |
| 8 | 11 | Forget Me Not - - - - - - - | Eden Kane | Decca |
| 13 | 12 | The Wanderer - - - - - - - | Dion | HMV |
| 15 | 13 | Softly As I Leave You - - - - - | Matt Monro | Parlophone |
| 14 | 14 | Hole In The Ground - - - - - - | Bernard Cribbins | Parlophone |
| 12 | 15 | Little Bitty Tear - - - - - - - | Burl Ives | Brunswick |
| — | 16 | Dream Baby - - - - - - - | Roy Orbison | London |
| 16 | 17 | I'll See You In My Dreams - - - | Pat Boone | London |
| — | 18 | Z Cars - - - - - - - - - | Johnny Keating | Picadilly |
| — | 19 | Twistin' The Night Away - - - - | Sam Cooke | RCA |
| — | 20 | Lesson One - - - - - - - - | Russ Conway | Columbia |

**Kenny:**

In 1962 the band appeared in *It's Trad, Dad!*, which was a film about the usual thing - 'Let's do the Show right here!' Helen Shapiro was the main star.

**John:**

*I always felt that* It's Trad, Dad *was trying to hedge its bets - despite its title, it made sure there was plenty of rock 'n' roll on the bill just in case the Trad Fad should evaporate before the film was released! The director, Dick Lester, certainly did all right for himself - he went on to direct two of the first Beatles films.*

*The film* Live It Up, *which was released in 1963, also featured the Kenny Ball Band, playing 'Rondo' (our 11th hit) and 'Hand Me Down My Walking Cane' (the B-side of what was to become our 12th). 'Rondo' was an adaption of 'Rondo Alla Turca' from Mozart's* Piano Sonata No.11 in A. *That sounds very posh, but in our free interpretation of*

Mozart's melody we made sure all potential difficulties were ironed out in advance. Hence, both the title and the tricky original key were changed to protect the innocent! To confound our critics at that time - who were now beginning to moan that trad jazz had had its day – 'Rondo' got to number 24 and stayed eight weeks in the NME charts.

Ken had a small acting role alongside David Hemmings in Live It Up, a film that NME described as "one hour's worth of story, 20 minutes of music". When NME asked Kenny how he felt about appearing in his second movie, Ken, with tongue in cheek, replied that he'd had to wait a long time for the right story and the right script!

Ken collected an armful of honours around this time: a Carl Alan award for Outstanding Trad Jazz Group of 1962 and a Broadcast Music Inc. of USA award for an 'outstanding achievement to music' ('Midnight in Moscow'). He came top of the US Billboard poll of dee-jays, who voted him leader of the 'Most Promising Band' and topped the Trumpet section of the British Melody Maker poll, while the band topped the NME poll. And at a ceremony held at the Hilton Hotel in July to publicise a forthcoming 'British Week' in the USA, Kenny was granted honorary citizenship of the birthplace of jazz, New Orleans.

But there was no let-up to the sniping in the music press, which continued to use provocative headlines such as 'Trad Boom Over …', 'Kenny Ball sounds the Last Post for Trad …', 'Trouble in Tradland …', and so forth. In answer to those critics who claimed that the band did not play jazz, Ken shrugged: "This gets me a bit cross … I disagree with what they say, but I'll defend to the death their right to say it."

***Kenny:***

Well, of course, in 1963 The Beatles arrived and everybody said, "The jazz thing's finished." And that was true for a lot of people. But I don't think we were really affected at all. And Acker Bilk says the same thing. Of course, we'd already had lots of hit records when The Beatles came along, and on one occasion when we played the Cavern Club in Liverpool – which, of course, had started out as a jazz club - The Beatles were our interval group.

### John:

*As a jazz club The Cavern was something else. The place steamed - literally. In fact, you could assess a band's popularity by the amount of fog generated by Cavern audiences. Well, not just from the audiences - much of it came from the gents' toilet; a deep trough, which on a crowded night often overflowed up to an inch deep on the stone floor. When the exit doors were opened wide at the end of a session vapour billowed out into the cobbled alley along with the leisurely departing audience, leaving passers-by with the impression that the place was on fire and no one could give a damn!*

*We were playing an all-nighter there in February 1961, when a group of young lads dressed in black leather came on stage to play rock music during the interval. At that time they called themselves The Silver Beatles and were still an amateur group. Our first impression was a bit snooty: we felt this was not the sort of act that should accompany a well-known professional jazz band like ours! Even so, we had to admit they were pretty good. I remember Ken saying to me at the time, "Look at that sparkle in their eyes - they've got real stage presence." The evidence was there right before us; we should've guessed that very soon they'd rise up and make the '60s their own.*

### Kenny:

We were lucky. It was only the singles - our hit singles - that more or less came to an end. All in all we had 13 in the Top Thirty, starting with 'Samantha' in 1961, which stayed in the Top Ten for 15 weeks, and ending with 'Hello Dolly', which got to number thirty after Louis had had the original hit. That stayed in the charts for seven weeks in, I think, June 1964. At that point we were on the Isle of Man doing cabaret and *Top of the Pops* made a film of us on Douglas seafront, where we mimed to our record on top of one of those horse-drawn trams that go up and down the promenade. Unfortunately, our record didn't get into the Top Twenty, which was the criterion for showing the film on *Top of the Pops*. There was also a version of 'Hello Dolly' by Frankie Vaughan – but, of course, Louis' was the main one. However, ours didn't do too badly. We also recorded a German version, with me reading the words phonetically, and an Italian one - and probably even one in Swahili, I think.

Later on I did a parody version called 'Hello Solly': "Hello Solly, well Hello Solly. It's Bah Mitzvah time, your son is now fourteen ...". Louis Benjamin, who was Jewish and one of the big cheeses of Pye Records, had that great Jewish sense of humour and he actually made a proper record of it and pressed a hundred copies. He even gave it a number; Pye Records 101S or something like that. Talk about laugh! Our last hit was 'When I'm 64', which, of course, came off The Beatles' *Sergeant Pepper* album. So we got our own back a bit! That was in 1967 and it made number 43 in the charts for a couple of weeks. Terry Lightfoot was with us then on clarinet. Dave Jones had left us after about eight years and Andy Cooper was yet to come. Maybe we tried too many different things later on, I don't know. But we carried on anyhow.

### John:
*And we kept making LPs, too. Our third album,* The Kenny Ball Show, *was from the Liverpool Empire, recorded live on April Fool's day 1961.*

### Kenny:
Paul McCartney was on that album! Well, he was in the audience, anyway. I've met him a few times since, and he told me he'd come along with his dad, and he said the concert was fantastic.

Afterwards I remember going home on the midnight train. It was a sleeper. I was in a cabin with Alan Freeman and one of his A&R crew, Les Cox. On the door of our compartment it said 'Ball, Cox and Freeman'.

### John:

*Our A&R man, Alan Freeman, had always wanted to record a live show with us. The Liverpool Empire was the ideal venue. The acoustics were good and it was a terrific concert. The show overran by half an hour and the audience was so enthusiastic they carried on stomping even after we'd played 'God Save the Queen', which in those days was always played at the end of a performance. To shout for more after the National Anthem had been played was unheard of - but we weren't complaining. Afterwards we listened to the playback and it sounded really good. Even though we'd played all our hits during the concert, none were featured on the album. Alan Freeman felt that the public could listen to our hits anytime they liked just by switching on their radios!*

### Kenny:

I've said it before: Alan Freeman was a lovely, lovely bloke. He was what I'd call … well, let's say he had a low sex drive. He fell in love with a lady who worked for Pye Records. And we were all surprised when he decided to get married. He went to live in Australia in the late '60s, and when we arrived in Sydney early one morning for a tour in 1970 he treated us to a grand champagne breakfast, with all the press and TV cameras there. He was a great man. And he produced all our hit records, every single one of them. And he was so proud of us. Alan at that time was on £30 a week. He never got a penny in royalties, which is amazing when you think about it - you know, a man with all those hit records under his belt. However, I'd take him out occasionally and thank him. In fact, I moved in with him once when I had a row with my first wife. He had a little flat in St

John's Wood.

While Alan was working in Australia I did a *This Is Your Life* programme, and the BBC offered to fly Alan back from Australia with his missus. And he came. And then, of course, once he was back here he decided to stay, and he got a job once again with Pye Records. I had Cyril Stapleton as an A&R man at that time, but Alan did work with us again. My brother-in-law decided that I should move from Pye to another company. But I was very loyal to Cyril Stapleton, who was the leader of the BBC Orchestra and was looking after me - for material and all that - and I couldn't leave him in the lurch. So I then fell out with my brother-in-law. We had a row and that was the end of our relationship for a while. But Alan and I stayed friends - you couldn't be anything else but friends with Alan.

Unfortunately, there's a bad ending to Alan's tale. We had an agent who looked after Alan as well as us, and late one night he took Alan home to his bungalow in Croydon, where he lived with his spouse. When Alan and the agent entered the bungalow there was nobody about, so Alan went upstairs to the bedroom, where he found his wife in bed with her boss - she was working for an insurance company. And, to show the sort of bloke Alan was, he said to her, "How could you do this to me? Not only that, you haven't fed the hamster!" There were shrieks of laughter all round - but the end result was they got divorced.

Of course, Alan wanted to see the children. He had two lovely kids, both of them very intelligent, and they still keep in contact with me. And his mum used to keep in touch with me, too - and his dad, who lived in Australia. But one day Alan went round to his ex-wife's house to see his children and while still in the car outside her house he had a heart attack and died. It was one of the saddest days of my life; he was such a dear friend. We played at his funeral, and just about everybody was there: Brian Matthew, Petula, our record boss Louis Benjamin ... I can't talk about it anymore, otherwise I'll start crying.

He was such a wonderful man, hit by such tragic circumstances. He's up in heaven somewhere, and I'm sure he's telling God how to run His record company!

### John:

*Whenever we'd recorded what we thought was a perfect take, Alan used to say, "Do one more, just for me, chaps." It was just his way of striving for perfection, but he'd kid us he was stockpiling these extra recordings for a special occasion. The special occasion he had in mind would be when our plane crashed into a mountain - like Buddy Holly's! Gleefully, he'd say that a posthumous Kenny Ball LP with a tastefully designed black border would provide his pension.*

*The band recorded with Pye Records for eight years, between May 1960 and March 1968. When the rights to the name Pye expired in 1980 the label changed its name to PRT, which stood for Precision Records and Tapes.*

*At the farewell party, held in the old studio where the band had recorded all its hits, I chatted with our sound engineer and asked whether I could have a rummage down in the vaults, where all the original tapes were kept. It was a real treasure trove. Down there on the shelves I found all the old tapes we'd recorded with Alan Freeman over the years. Quite a few had never been released. Among them was a very rare tape for an album we'd recorded for Japanese Pye during a tour of Japan in 1964. It'd been sent to London 'for reference', I suppose, as it wasn't issued in Britain at the time. The sound engineer, whom we knew well from our days with Pye records, kindly made a couple of cassette tapes of this album for Ken and myself. Many years later that Japanese album resurfaced in a CD collection - the box set of Pye's early Kenny Ball jazz LPs.*

*I thought back to when we recorded that session in Japan. We'd gone into the Tokyo recording studios of Japanese Pye on the morning of 29 November 1964. Our hosts had asked for an album of 12 titles, all of which must be finished that day. The band was a bit frazzled, owing to a series of late nights, long journeys and too much Nikka whisky (not to be recommended in great quantities!) and by lunchtime we had only three numbers in the can. To help us relax, the producer sent us out for a meal at a Chinese restaurant. After we'd eaten and the dishes had been removed, a waiter placed an ashtray on the now empty central turntable. Maybe it was the liberal supply of saki that made us all focus closely on that ashtray. Anyway, someone casually spun the turntable and all our eyes followed the ashtray as it circulated. It put us in mind of a ball rolling round a roulette wheel. Someone then had the bright idea that we should all lob a 20-yen coin into that ashtray, set it spinning, and the nearest person to the kitty when it stopped moving could claim it. Good game; and it kept us occupied for, well, maybe an hour or two. Certainly by the time we left that restaurant dusk had fallen and some of us were completely skint!*

*Our Japanese recording engineer was waiting patiently for us at the door of his studio. He was far too polite to criticise us for being late. Instead, he greeted us with a bow and thanked us for being so thoughtful as to allow him plenty of time to adjust the recording balance to his satisfaction.*

*By midnight we were nearly through in more ways than one. Empty beer bottles littered the floor of the studio, and Ken had in the meantime switched to Japanese brandy, which - so he informed everyone - medicinally heightened his creative powers. Earlier our pianist Ron Weatherburn had tried this same magic elixir, which should've been a warning sign - Ron had now turned into a hopelessly giggling paralytic. Fortunately, none of the weird goings-on in that studio are evident on the final recording, the high spot of which was the tune we'd deliberately saved until last: our version of the theme to the film* **Bridge Over the River Kwai.** *This well-known ditty, better known as 'Colonel Bogey' (or by its unofficial title, 'Bollocks and the Same to You'), had been specifically requested by our Japanese hosts. Luckily, they didn't catch the subtle nuances of its alternative lyrics when we raucously sang it to them* *at the end of the session!*

*Talking about not understanding lyrics reminds me of a strange episode concerning our next pianist, John Parker, which occurred during our second tour of Japan in 1972. The band had finished the night's concert in Tokyo, and our hosts had taken us to a small drinking club in which to relax after hours, as it were. Parker, having seen a piano on the small stage, went up and tickled the ivories for a bit, then entertained the audience with some sedate cocktail music. After a while, as the booze began to flow, his cocktail music turned into ragtime, then into a strident 'Mrs Mills' session, and finally a singalong of bawdy ditties of which only John Parker knew the words. "Come along, come along, all together now," he urged his listeners. Under John's direction, his obedient Japanese audience, after struggling with the unfamiliar lyrics, soon enthusiastically joined in the refrain:*

*"Ring the bell verger, ring the bell ring* (they trilled)
*Perhaps the congregation will condescend to sing,*
*Perhaps the FUCKING organist will sit upon his stool,*
*And play the FUCKING organ, not his FUCKING tool!"*

### Kenny:

By the mid-sixties the club scene was changing. All the jazz clubs had shut down, so we switched to playing the cabaret rooms, which were a pain in the arse, but that was the thing to do in those days. They were called cabaret clubs, but the entertainment was only there to attract the punters to spend their money gambling. We played one spot nightly in each club, and because there were so many clubs around we used to 'double' - that is, do our first spot, then pack up quickly to get to another club in a different town for our next spot. We might start with an 8 p.m. show in Burnley and then dash across to Blackpool, which is about 50 miles away, to play from 11 to 12. We'd have about two hours between gigs and that was all.

Around the Newcastle area there were at least half a dozen clubs. We could start off in Middlesbrough and end up in Redcar on the same night. Another one was South Shields; and Batley, of course, where Louis Armstrong played in 1969.

One of the funniest venues was the Working Men's Club in Greasborough, near Rotherham in Yorkshire. We were on the bill with Danny Williams, who'd had a great big hit with 'Moon River' back in November 1961. We were asked to play a short version of our show at lunchtime, just so the punters could see how good we were and assess whether they were going to come back to see us during the week or not. So we did our lunchtime spot, and the manager came up and said, "That's fine, Mr Kenny Ball and you lads. Thank you very much. I'll put you top of the bill tonight." Now Danny Williams - who was a lovely chap, with a good voice as well - was supposed to be top of the bill and he was shaken. But the manager said to him, "No, I don't want you. Just go to the office and you'll get paid off. You don't have to worry about anything - you'll get your money." And that was that.

### John:

*Finding out that a fellow artiste has been paid off is a bit unsettling, especially when you're about to go on stage. Dave Jones, outwardly an easy-going and relaxed chap, was prone to bouts of nervous tension just before a gig, and this news did him no good at all. Midway through his solo spot in 'High Society', Ken and I both saw that Dave was about to throw up, so we tried to help out with a bit of ensemble playing. Dave frowned to show us he didn't need our assistance, then revved up into top gear, playing his heart out in chorus after chorus. The audience went wild. Dave deserved a medal for that. The DFC - Damn Fine Clarinettist!*

**Kenny:**

Another ridiculous thing I'll never forget as long as I live was on another lunchtime show at that Greasborough club. A comedian came on and he went down like a lead balloon. Afterwards the club secretary came on and said, "Excuse me, ladies and gentlemen, I'd like to call a minute's silence for Mr Hargreaves who's passed away. He was a member of the committee, as I'm sure you all know. So okay, lads, start the silence now." Of course, everyone was jabbering and there was no silence at all. The secretary got very annoyed and shouted, "Eh up. Now look 'ere. If you don't give me a minute's silence, I'll bring that bloody comedian back on."

**John:**

*As well as cabaret clubs, we often played for dances at Mecca ballrooms, most of which had a revolving stage. The house band would be playing out front while we set up behind the curtain and waited for the changeover. If all went well, the mechanism would start up; the house band would then circle gently and return backstage while the Kenny Ball band emerged out front, all guns blazing. More often than not, however, things didn't run so smoothly. On one occasion the microphone wiring got caught in the gap as we revolved. As the tension of the wires increased, we had to jump like schoolgirls with a skipping rope. All the mikes got taken out first, then part of the drum kit, and finally the drummer too! Another time the stage didn't stop revolving, and the audience were treated to a brief glimpse of the Kenny Ball Band giving their all in 'Jazz Band Ball' before the surprised house band re-emerged again; or some of them anyway - only those who were still on stage packing up their instruments or sipping their pints. On a third occasion the stage stopped halfway, showing a side-on view of both bands. That time the mechanism started up again and accelerated without stopping. Those of us who were fairly nimble had to seize their chance each time the stage returned behind the curtains to leap to safety.*

*Kenny:*

By now we were touring non-stop with cabaret dates, nightclubs, dances and concerts, and in 1968 we played four concerts with Louis Armstrong and his All Stars. So, even though the pop scene had destroyed the jazz club scene, we hardly noticed any other differences; we were still doing well.

Louis Armstrong? Yes, it was great to meet him. He was very nice, especially when he said I was a genius! We did the shows with him and his band in London: two at Hammersmith Palais and two at Victoria. I remember trumpet player Spike Mackintosh being there on the first night - he was one of the great British jazz characters and the father of Cameron Mackintosh, who's produced all the big shows with Andrew Lloyd Webber. Well, Spike was a reasonable Louis Armstrong imitator, not a brilliant trumpet player, but Louis Armstrong was everything to him. He met me in the pub before the show and said, "Please, please get me into Louis' dressing room," to which I replied, "Well come into the theatre with me." So we walked in together, chatting like old friends, and then he went off looking for Louis. Although he somehow managed to get himself lost in the passageways under the stage, he did eventually find his hero to say hello. I heard later that he'd slept all night in the theatre because he'd got pissed and couldn't remember where he'd parked his car!

Well, there'll never be another one like Louis Armstrong. Back in the 1920s he left New Orleans for Chicago, joined the King Oliver orchestra and became famous. Just like that. While he was still playing with King Oliver he also recorded what they call the Hot 5's and Hot 7's - small group bands, which are now classics. Sometimes I feel - or I know - that some of his solos cannot be beaten. You can try, but you can't get better than Louis and I don't think anyone ever will. Even his improvisations on record now seem to have become part of the tune itself.

Later he became involved in the commercial side of jazz, fronting a big band. He still had that same silvery tone and the same great ideas, except that he was now playing the tunes of the day. That's something that I and the boys in my band also emulated in the early '60s with 'Samantha' and one or two other songs. But, at the same time, one of the Top Ten hits we had in the '60s was 'Someday You'll be Sorry', a song written by Louis many years earlier.

We first met Louis face-to-face when he was over here in 1962. He presented me and the guys with our gold disc for 'Midnight in Moscow'. I think he'd prepared his lines: "We're having a ball with Mr Ball" type of thing.

Then in 1968 he came over to play at the Batley Variety Club, followed by those four concerts in London. At the New Victoria Theatre we came on stage first and opened up with something like 'South Rampart Street Parade'. Bill Bowyer, our roadie, was standing in the wings yelling, "Give it crutch!" like he always did - although I think on this night he was using the testicular version! Louis was standing next to him side-stage, in his dressing gown, clocking us. He said to Bill Bowyer - and I've only got Bill's word for this: "This man's a genius." I wish I could've heard those words. Then he came rushing on stage and embraced me. It was the first time the audience had seen Louis - and here he was, on stage in his white dressing gown. Everyone went bananas. What an incredible way to meet the man you idolise.

The second two concerts were at the Hammersmith Odeon - now the Apollo. Funnily enough, I remember him in his dressing room going on about this stuff called Swiss Kriss - it was a herbal laxative, and Louis swore by it. He even had a picture taken of himself sitting on the loo, which he used as his publicity shot. I think Swiss Kriss must've been his sponsor at that time.

**John:**

*July 4th was Louis' 68th birthday, and on the morning before his (and our) second pair of concerts at the Hammersmith Odeon the Daily Express arranged a birthday bash for Louis. It was held at the Savoy Hotel in, appropriately, the Abraham Lincoln room.*

*The Kenny Ball band, having welcomed Louis' arrival with our version of 'A Closer Walk With Thee', were seated in a prime position at the front, and all Louis' sidemen were alongside us. Louis' trombonist, Tyree Glenn, was sitting next to me. He was a rather large chap, and apparently Louis had got him on Swiss Kris to lose some weight. If so, it wasn't yet working. During lunch I had a chance to share a few jovial words with Tyree. He proclaimed himself an Anglophile and said he was in love with our Queen.*

*"She wears Union Jack knickers, you know," I told him.*

*"Is that true?" he breathed. "Man, I could **eat** my way through those!"*

**Kenny:**

Louis always had his doctor accompanying him, bless his heart. He'd started to deteriorate then, as we'd seen on some of the TV broadcasts. It happens to everybody, I'm afraid. You can't keep going forever. I have a personal opinion about his deterioration. It started quite early in his early sixties. I think it had something to do with marijuana. It's all very well to say marijuana is harmless, but it does affect the brain. It's like drink. If it continues over a lifetime, I think it leads to deterioration in your mental faculties. So to say it doesn't do any harm is quite frankly a load of bollocks. But there you go.

We loved Louis. And he's inspired every jazz musician since. Even the modernists and the ultra-modernists recognise his contribution to jazz, either musically, or through entertainment. He's an example of how to carry yourself and treat people with dignity. He was popular in areas where it was forbidden for black people to go. I think he started to transcend the barriers of that awful colour bar very early on. It still happens, though. We had experience of it when we first went to New Orleans. I saw some little kid dancing in the street, and an adult urging him on: "Go on, dance for the man." And there's the back of the bus thing, and having to use different toilets and water fountains. It was abhorrent to us because we were inspired by those people, the great jazz musicians, whether they were black, brown, pink or striped. What matters is what's inside.

Louis died in 1971 and everyone was upset. There were headlines about it in all the papers. He did a solo appearance over here just before he died, but he wasn't well. Somebody told me that he'd tried to climb on a stage to play, but it was pathetic. So perhaps it was time for him to give up. I've no intention myself - one never knows what's around the corner, does one?

Louis wrote me a letter after that short tour with us. He'd gone back to the USA and was playing at Lake Tahoe at the time. In his letter he said, "I shall never forget our engagement together. Regards to all of your boys, (Satch) Louis Armstrong."

*Evening News, 5 July 1968:*

## WHAT A WONDERFUL NIGHT FOR SATCHMO
**By STANLEY REED**

*Kenny Ball's Jazzmen were going all out in their last number at the Odeon, Hammersmith, when, in the wings, I caught a glimpse of Louis Armstrong, a wide beam of appreciation stretching from ear to ear. That's how it was at the 68th birthday concert of Satchmo and his All Stars. A smile spread across the face of the packed audience and stayed there - an audience that ranged from youngsters under 10 to youngsters over 60. Louis was their darling; an amazing symbol of the young-in-heart; who has set so many barriers tumbling and has long been a legend in his lifetime.*

*He played and sang "Dolly", "Cabaret" and "Blueberry Hill" and the crowd loved every note, every rasping syllable.*

*There were big hands too for trombonist Tyree Glenn, George Catlett on bass, drummer Danny Barcelona and Joe Nuranyi on clarinet.*

*Altogether a pleasing session which the Kenny Ball band got going very well. Like Louis they know that to get Jazz going these days you've got to be entertaining with it.*

# 7
# THE TV YEARS

*Kenny:*

In the late 1950s and early '60s Alma Cogan's TV show was very, very popular. We were due to appear on it and they asked Alma if she'd present us with a silver disc for 'March of the Siamese Children'. It was number one in the hit parade and we'd sold a quarter of a million records. This was the night that Frankie Howerd made his comeback on that same show, and Frankie took off from there and never looked back after that. Alma had a bubbling personality. And she knew her stagecraft, because she upstaged me something terrible. She said, "And now, Kenny, I'd like to present you with this silver disc - come along, Kenny." And so I went on stage and was walking towards her, and she was holding the silver disc more or less away from me. By the way, 'upstaging' is when you never turn your face or body away from the camera. I was beautifully upstaged by Alma Cogan, because being a trumpet player I didn't know much about stagecraft. "Here you are, Kenny," she said, and I had to walk round her, because she was still facing the camera while I had my back to it while trying to get hold of that silver disc!

Des O'Connor was a great upstager. Des had started off as Lonnie Donegan's warm-up man on his show, *Putting on the Donegan*. Anyway, we were on a *Sunday Night at the Palladium* show and Des wanted to do a duet with me, so that's what we did. And Des upstaged me, which was very funny. On Des's shows there was always a camera on him - full face, never on the side or behind. So Des and I were on the stage, standing side by side, and he was doing all the upstaging bit while we were singing a song called 'Blues My Naughty Sweetie'. I didn't get angry; I started laughing, because I realised what he was trying to do. And so I did it the opposite way.

Funnily enough, if you watch Bing Crosby and Bob Hope you'll see they played that game, too. The one that got away with it the most was Eric Morecambe, because he looked straight at the camera, very intensely. This turned everything around completely, as, of course, you follow the movement. So Eric Morecambe had the ideal remedy for anyone that might try to upstage him.

### John:

*The band used to do the ATV television show,* Sunday Night at the London Palladium, *quite often in the early '60s. The format for the show never altered; it opened with high kicks from the Tiller Girls and a welcome from the host, who at that time was Norman Vaughan. The Kenny Ball Band's spot was in the first half, before 'Beat the Clock'. At the end of the second half, following the star turn, came the finale in which all the acts gathered and waved goodbye from the famous revolving stage.*

*As we were always on in the first half, we used to play our number and then whip out through the stage door to the Shakespeare pub across the road. While in there we had to keep our eye on the clock, because all the acts had to return on stage for the finale.*

*The finale was a set piece in which a set of two-foot high styrofoam spangly letters were arranged in a circle like Stonehenge, spelling out 'Sunday Night at the Palladium'.*

*Everyone in the cast had been allotted their own letter in advance, and in the four-minute ad break before the finale we all located our respective letter and stood behind it. When the curtain went up, the stage revolved and everyone waved to the audience as they went round.*

*This was fine, except for one occasion when guitarist/banjoist Paddy*

*Lightfoot and I forgot to check our watches while in the Shakespeare, and in a panic we ran into the theatre and charged onto the stage - which by that time had started revolving. We then stumbled around, bumping into each other, trying to find our respective letters. What made it worse was the fact that we'd just lit up a large cigar each, and in our haste to get on stage we'd forgotten to take them out of our mouths.*

*The TV camera situated high up in the gods captured the scene: Paddy and me zig-zagging around in the centre of the circle like a manic pair of Groucho Marxes. In its heyday 28 million viewers tuned in, which meant our daft performance must've been observed by nearly half the population of the United Kingdom! Fortunately, no one has ever mentioned it. They must've thought it was part of the act!*

### Kenny:

And then Eric Morecambe and Ernie Wise came along. In early 1968 Eric and Ernie were doing a series of black and white TV shows for ITV, and they always featured a jazz band - us, Chris Barber, Acker Bilk, Alex Welsh - all the famous jazz bands from the Trad Boom days. In fact, if you look on YouTube we're on there from one of those early shows. Anyhow, that series was coming to an end and we were asked to go back to do the last show. Sid Green and Dick Hill were the scriptwriters then. We became friendly with them and they told me, "You're definitely the best band."

So I went up to the Green Room afterwards to have a quiet drink, and Sid and Dick appeared and said, "Can we have a word with you, Ken?"

"Yes, of course," I said.

"It was absolutely wonderful. Thanks ever so much," they reiterated.

At this point Eric and Ernie came over and said, "We're going over from ATV to the BBC. Would you like to come with us?"

Well, what would you say?

The show was in colour on BBC (ATV was still black and white then), plus Eric Morecambe and Ernie Wise were already being watched by 20 million people. And in a world that was completely dominated by pop music, that was no bad thing.

So we started a series in the late '60s and appeared on it every week from then on, airing on BBC1 at 8.15 every Saturday night. My clarinettist Andy Cooper had joined us by then.

### John:

*Andy Cooper joined us on clarinet from the Alan Elsdon band in November 1967. His first gig with us was, fittingly, on the* Lord Mayor's Show. *The band was featured on the British Motor Corporation display, in which each band member stood on a separate mini-moke float alongside one of the current Miss World contestants. It was a cold morning, and the band turned up well prepared in thick woollen sweaters. The Miss World contestants, on the other hand, wore only their bikinis and goose pimples. Pictured in retrospect, our stately procession that morning through the streets of the City of London strikes me as more than a little bizarre: seven Mini Moke pick-ups moving at walking speed in perfect formation; seven gorgeous girls; seven lecherous jazz musicians - under such conditions it was a miracle that 'Muskrat Ramble' never missed a beat. I remember casting a surreptitious glance around me at this curious scene and meeting, for the first time, the owl-eyed stare of our new clarinettist. I had a hunch then, which would soon be proved right, that with Andy Cooper in the band life would never be quite the same again!*

### Kenny:

Eric and Ernie really were naturally funny men. It's hard to say who was really the boss. Anyhow, they always did three rehearsals during the day, ending up with a dress rehearsal, and we always sat in the front seats watching them. We never realised this at the time, but they used us as a kind of sounding board - if we laughed at one of their gags it was certainly kept in, and if we didn't laugh then something else was put in its place.

I remember Eric walking on stage while Ron Bowden was sitting there at his drums, and lifting up Ron's big cymbal, peering under it as if it were a saucepan lid and saying, "Stew again?"

Another time Ernie introduced us with the words, "Ladies and Gentlemen, the Kenny Ball Jazzmen."

"Not them again," said Eric.

"Yes, they're very good," Ernie responded.

So Eric said, "I know what it is - they've found where you buried your wallet."

We fell about laughing in our front row seats, so they kept that in the show, naturally.

Then on another of the shows we came on in our swimming trunks but were hiding behind the piano, so it looked as if we were all in the nude. I think there's a picture of that somewhere. It might've been on the back of a record.

And were they perfectionists! They used to rehearse and rehearse and rehearse. Eric was a stickler for detail, but then once they knew the routine back to front they could ad lib if they wanted to, or if a mistake was made. The shows were live - or I should say we used to record them 'live', i.e., in front of an audience, on a Wednesday, and the show would be broadcast the following Sunday. Of course, if there was a mistake they could always edit it out or do the scene again.

We had two producers on the show and the second one, John Ammonds, was fierce, and also very strict if the slightest thing went wrong. For some reason he didn't like our banjoist, Ted Baldwin, who joined us in 1970 when Paddy Lightfoot left the band. Ted wasn't photogenic, he said; he had freckles and a scar as well and he didn't smile a lot. So he was out of favour. But, although he was strict, he wasn't unpleasant, and had we made a small mistake in the number we were playing I really don't think he would've spotted it. In fact, we never had to replay a number the whole time we were on the show - although we were certainly pretty jittery because of all the tension in the air. On one occasion Paddy Lightfoot, who played banjo with us throughout the hit years, had to sing 'Blues My Naughty Sweetie Gave to Me'. In the middle there's a kind of novelty vocal; the tempo's doubled-up with a lot of very fast words. It wasn't the kind of thing to tackle when you've had a drink or two - and you could see Paddy sweating. But he got through it okay and we never had to do anything again.   That's amazing, thinking about it.

However, John Ammonds was very influential in Eric and Ernie's success. It was his idea to have the celebrity guests on the show and he also invented their famous dance at the end of the show.

This is how we did the show. First of all, at the end of the show we'd just done we had to play to John Ammonds the tune we were going to do the following week, so I had to have that arrangement ready. And it had to be entertaining and lively, which is understandable for a comedy programme - you can't sing a doom-laden blues. So that was the first thing. If we were involved in any comedy sketches we had to go to rehearsals somewhere in West London. I remember it being very cold there at 10 o'clock in the morning, and nothing seemed funny at all to us. But Eric and Ernie were very serious about their comedy. For our part, we had to write out every band routine to the letter. For example, there might be an 8-bar introduction, followed by a band ensemble and then, say, a 32-bar vocal with accompaniment by clarinet or trombone or whatever. All of it had to be detailed. Of course, they had to know exactly what we were going to do in advance in order to get the camera shots worked out.

Once everything had been sorted out, we'd arrive at the studios on the day, and there might be two or three run-throughs to get the camera shots exactly right. Once all that was done, all we had to do was simply play, and maybe give the cameraman a couple of extra little ideas - come in on the clarinet here maybe; or try not to film anyone picking their nose -that sort of thing. Of course, as the routine was worked out and timed to the second, you couldn't just throw in an extra chorus for someone if things were going well.

One quite important thing, from the continuity point of view, was that they used two stages. Eric and Ernie used to start the whole show off, and their stage had a gold curtain at the back. Then on the other stage - which was to the right as you looked from the audience - the guest artist would do their number while Eric and Ernie went off to change their trousers or get into another costume or whatever. So the whole thing was continuous. They might have a warm-up comedian, too, who would say something along the lines of, "Oh, Ernie and Eric will be back in just a second." Also, of course, if they had a kitchen sketch or one of their famous bedroom sketches, which Eddie Brabin introduced, the scene on their side of their stage could be changed while the guest artists did their number. Sometimes small five-minute sketches had already been filmed, so they could be slipped in where needed.

So recording the show was fun, but you really had to concentrate – although, having spent a lot of time during the day up in the bar on the seventh floor, we all used to get fairly out of our heads at the same time. Nowadays, it might seem nerve-racking, but we were young then, and it didn't feel so at the time. So we had a great four years.

Then in November 1971 we heard that we'd been dropped from the show, because Eric and Ernie were moving to ITV. And

Above left: Kenny Ball in 1940 aged 10

Above right: John Bennett in 1940 aged 4

Below: The Kenny Ball Band 1959, back in London and 'really going'

Dickie Bishop in a trance. Ken is wondering why he can't hear the banjo

In the studios

Above: Alan A. Freeman and Kenny

Right: The band in 1961. Back Row: Ron Weatherburn, Vic Pitt, John Bennett, Clinton Ford, Bill Dixon (banjo), Ron Bowden. In front: Dave Jones, Kenny

Left: Midnight in Moscow

Below: Kenny and John Bennett at the Cavern, Liverpool

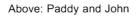

Above: Paddy and John

Right: A clean-cut Andy Cooper at one of his first gigs with the band

Left: Kenny Ball and *Her* Jazzmen

Below: Arrival in Japan 1964

Above: Rolf Harris Shows John
how to play the didgeridoo

Right: Doll and Pop Ball

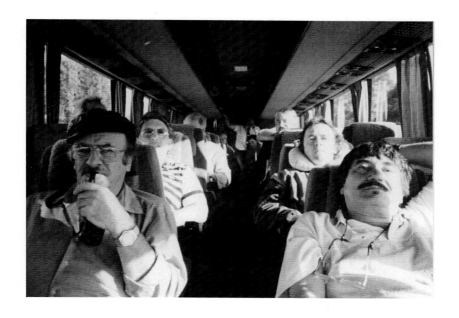

Above: Crossing the Nullarbor, Acker and Kenny

Below: Better out than in – Ron Bowden (left) and John Benson (right)

BEAT IT:
Sacked
drummer
Ron

Above: The Band in the 50's. L-R Colin Bates, Dave Jones, Brian Prudence, Kenny, Tony Budd, John Bennett, John Potter

Below: The Band in the 60's. At rear, Paddy Lightfoot (banjo), Kenny, Ron Weatherburn. At front, Dave Jones, Ron Bowden, John Bennett, Vic Pitt

## KENNY BALL and the JAZZMEN

Above: The Band in the 70's. L-R Ron Bowden, Ted Baldwin (banjo), Vic Pitt, John Parker (piano), John Bennett, Andy Cooper, Kenny

Below: The Band in the 80's. L-R John Bennett, Andy Cooper, Tony Pitt (banjo/Guitar). Kenny, John Benson (bass), Ron Bowden, Duncan Swift (piano)

Above: The Band in the 90's. L-R John Benson, John Fenner (banjo/Guitar), Ron Bowden, Kenny, Andy Cooper, John Bennett, Hugh Ledigo (piano)

Below: The Band in the 00's. L-R John Bennett, Hugh Ledigo, Nivk Millward (drums), Kenny, Bill Coleman (bass), Andy Cooper

that was the biggest mistake they ever made. With the BBC they had two good producers - John Ammonds and Ernest Maxin - who got on well with everyone and who believed in the Hollywood musical type of thing. They wanted an extravaganza on every programme and the BBC didn't mind spending money and, as it was just BBC London back then, they seemed to have plenty to spend. They were getting some incredible viewing figures and I suppose they got their licence fees and didn't have hundreds of other regional stations to finance. So I think it was all a matter of money in the end. ITV didn't pay for extra musicians, although they did, of course, have a band on the show. And I think they cut the show down to half an hour, whereas we'd had 45 minutes with the BBC. So everything definitely went downhill. It was a great shame.

During our time on the show we saw the incredible change that came about after Sid and Dick left and Eddie Brabin came in. He was a genius; the man responsible for changing Eric and Ernie's characters around. Eric had been the bumbling one to begin with, but he ended up the smart one. And that was a great idea, which took the two of them right to the top. All those shows were hilarious - and now they've turned into classics. Who could forget Glenda Jackson playing Cleopatra, or André Previn in the wonderful sketch with the concert orchestra and Ernie playing (or trying to play) the Grieg piano concerto? The funny part about that was that the orchestra couldn't see what was going on; they were behind the curtain while André was doing the cross-talk with Eric and Ernie. The sketch was front-of-curtain and done without any rehearsal with André - or 'Mr Preview' as Ernie kept calling him. Apparently, he'd learned the whole script in his taxi on the way to the studio. They went through it with just a read-through only and then André did it off the cuff, just like that. It was marvellous, and it's a shame that we didn't even get to meet André - he was literally in and out.

Come to think about it, we hardly ever saw the orchestra during our time with the show. They were somewhere out back, even though they were all wearing evening dress. But I remember one time Johnny Parker was sitting at the piano tinkering away on something from Rachmaninoff when the orchestra pianist, a foreign gentleman, strode up very grandly in his white tie and tails and said, "If you *must* play zis, play it in ze right key!" With that, he nudged Johnny off the piano stool, took his place and played the thing with all its flourishes from beginning to end. Then, without a word, he got up and disappeared behind the scenes.

As for the guest stars, well of course there were dozens - everyone from Englebert Humperdinck to Bob Monkhouse, and all the current pop stars too. I fell in love with Nina of 'Nina and Frederick'; she was lovely, very beautiful. We had a drink afterwards together and - put it this way - my hormones were working overtime when she was there. I don't remember anyone being 'objectionable', as it were. Frankie Vaughan used to come on the show occasionally and could be a bit nervy, but the actors were always good fun. I'd like to see some of those early shows again now, but some of the old film reels have been destroyed. Also, when they got around to using videotape it was so expensive that they wiped our shows in order to use the tapes again.

**John:**
*The good news is that some of those Eric and Ernie shows did survive and since being rediscovered they've been issued as BBC DVD sets. The ones on which the Kenny Ball Band appears are Series 1 and 2, Series 3, Series 4, Series 5, Series 6 and the Christmas Specials. Each set contains two DVDs apart from the Christmas set, which comprises three.*

**Kenny:**

In 1971 Eamonn Andrews caught me on *This Is Your Life*. Unbeknown to me, for weeks there'd been TV people in touch with my wife Betty and all the band, gathering information for the show. On the day in question we were returning to London on the train from Glasgow. At the time I thought, this is very nice. The stationmaster in Glasgow had seen us onto the train in person, which made me feel very important. Anyhow, as far as I knew I had a gig at the Dorchester Hotel in London. It was put to me that this would be a private function, and I was prepared for that. Even so, I was a bit worried: it looked as if we were going to get there only just in time. On the train, every time I looked for the guys in the band I'd find them propping up the bar and looking a little shifty. This seemed a bit odd, so I said, "Look here, chaps, I'm all for having a drink or two, but we've got a very important charity function at the Dorchester tonight."

Anyway, we arrived at Euston's platform five and I got off the train. I could see floodlights and TV cameras up at the front end, but didn't think anything of it. While on the train I remembered spotting the Post Office Union chap, Tom Jackson - the one with the huge handlebar moustache - and as there was an ongoing postal strike at this time I thought all the ballyhoo was for him.

So I started to walk past the cameras, but they followed me round. I was a bit embarrassed, trying to hide a magazine I was carrying that had rude things in it - *Playboy*, I think. Suddenly a bloke wearing a railway inspector's peaked cap appeared in front of me - and it was Eamonn Andrews. I did the OMG bit! And then it all fell into place. It was me they were after, not Tom Jackson. And I was going to be on *This Is Your Life*!

Unfortunately, this was in the days before video recorders were all the rage, so I don't have it on film - but I do have the red book! I also have an LP recording of the show. All my family were there: my dad, my brothers and sisters. Eamonn introduced Dad as an "83-year-old former all-in wrestler and piccolo player," and asked him how that "rare combination" came about. Dad replied, "Simply because we lived in a district where sometimes it was very necessary to combine the two." It sounded very dignified and everyone laughed. Joe Brown turned up, and Lonnie Donegan was there on a live link from Manchester - which was very technically modern for that period. At that time we were still doing the Eric and Ernie shows, but this was ITV and Eric and Ernie were on the BBC. I think ITV did try to get them on the show, but I don't think the BBC would allow it. One of the high spots was my brother Ted telling how he used to come home in the evening when I was courting my first wife Betty. He'd say, "What's it to be tonight, Ken? Trumpet or crumpet?" That really brought the house down. Unfortunately, all my brothers and sisters that were on that show have since died, and I'm now the last one left of the original nine.

After the show there was a party at the Marquee - a Soho jazz club of which I was part founder. What sticks in my mind there is our drummer Ron Bowden finding the top session drummer of that time, Phil Seaman, just lying in the gutter outside the back entrance. Ron brought him inside. To see Phil - once the very best of British drummers - now reduced to this was awful. He'd lost all his teeth, could hardly talk, and was trying to stuff coleslaw in his mouth with his bare hands. Bloody heroin! Bastard drugs.

**John:**
*One important guest that we tried, and failed, to get on Kenny's* This Is Your Life *programme was Karlheinz Drechsel, a jazz radio presenter from East Germany. Karlheinz had accompanied us from city to city on*

*previous tours out there. He always introduced our shows with a long preamble that the audience seemed to think was very funny, although as none of the band were quick enough at translating German to English we never found out what he was saying about us. But we considered him a mate and his radio jazz programme was the high spot of the week for Eastern Bloc jazz lovers. The programmers for* This Is Your Life *planned to spring Karlheinz out of East Germany just for a day, so he could appear on the show as a guest. However, the East German authorities wouldn't hear of it and refused to give him a visa, so ITV risked sending in a team to film an interview with Karlheinz secretly on his home ground. But as they were about to leave East Germany the team was intercepted, their film was confiscated, and Karlheinz's punishment for that indiscretion, we learned later, was to be demoted from whatever political rank he was holding at that time. Fortunately, the collapse of the Berlin Wall put everything to rights, and now 80-year-old Karlheinz Drechsel is once again Germany's voice of jazz.*

### *Kenny:*

Not long after our stint on the Eric and Ernie TV shows we were fortunate to be offered a residency on *Saturday Night at the Mill*. We got to know the people on that show very well, because we did about four or five series between 1976 and 1981. The show was produced in Birmingham by Roy Ronnie and directed by Roy Norton (they were known as the 'two Roys') and in our time there were several presenters, including Bob Langley, Tony Lewis, Donny McLeod and Jenny Hanley. There were absolutely hundreds of famous guests, old and new. You name them and they were there: Nana Mouskouri, Peter Ustinov, Billy Dainty, Stirling Moss, Dusty Springfield, James Last, Sheila Hancock, Burl Ives, Ginger Rogers. We played for Ginger Rogers' dance routine with Bob Langley! Then there was Natalie Wood, Dennis Waterman, Spike Milligan, racing driver James Hunt, Chesney Allen from Flanagan and Allen, and

Sandy Powell, who was one of the funniest men I've ever seen. He would start singing with his hands by his sides, and then he'd raise them outwards and his arms would gradually get longer and longer until they were each about ten feet long. I don't think I've ever laughed so much in my life! There were dozens of amazing acts and I don't remember anyone being stand-offish in any way at all; they'd all join us up at the bar - people like Omar Sharif, Michael Caine, just about everyone.

For *Saturday Night at the Mill* everybody was called in for various rehearsals at 11 o'clock or 12 noon. The show went out live around 12 hours later, at 11 p.m., and during that time the Green Room was open, offering lots of food and all the wine, beer and spirits you could possibly drink. So you can guess what happened with some of the guests. Oliver Reed was hilarious. When it was time for him to come on he just went to the side of the stage and stood still. He had to walk right in front of us to get on set while we were playing 'There's No Business Like Show Business, but he just couldn't move. He'd decided he wasn't going to go on. So after we'd played the tune at least half a dozen times my wife Michelle, together with the floor lady, got hold of him and gave him a great big shove. He went flying across the set, collapsed on the chair, and then stood up and took his trousers off. And this was live TV! Lovely chap.

It was in March 1977 that Norman Wisdom was on the show. On the main part of his act he was dressed in a one-man-band outfit, with drums attached to his chest and cymbals strapped to his knees. It went fine in rehearsal, but when he was being dressed on the night someone for a joke strapped the cymbals to the outside of his legs! And Norman hadn't noticed. So, of course, he was banging his knees together with no cymbal clash. Another part of the act involved him running in from outside and crashing through a glass door - one made of harmless sugar glass. However, Norman somehow managed to crash into the solid plate glass of the real door alongside it! It really wasn't poor old Norman's night, because on top of everything else his flies were wide open. Obviously he didn't know, and somebody must've phoned the floor manager about it. All kinds of panicky offstage signs were made to him, but he didn't take any notice. He finished his interview, walked over to me and said, "What we gonna do now, Ken?" And I replied, "Before we do anything, we'd better do this," and I stretched over and pulled his zip up, prompting a big cheer from the audience. Norman certainly remembers the story, because later he mentioned it in his autobiography. And he had a neat line to follow it: "I used to be a flyweight champion" - which was actually true!

We had some other amazing scenes. A chap named Sandy Russell - a Scotsman with a broad Glaswegian accent - was a big fan of our band. He was there on the night Andy Williams was on the show. There'd been a big case in the papers recently concerning Andy Williams' wife, who'd been accused of murder but was later released from the charge. After the show had ended, Andy - a real American smoothie - came up to me and said, "Oh yeah, great music. Enjoyed that music, Kenny." And then along came Sandy: "Oh, there you are, Mr Williams. Very nice singing. Now, for God's sake, how did you get your wife off that bloody murder charge - how much did you have to pay?" Andy Williams wasn't very amused.

On the show we tried to get people to do things they weren't known for - like James Hunt, who won the Formula One World Championship in 1976, playing trumpet with us. Another was astronomer Patrick Moore, presenter of *The Sky at Night*, who played great xylophone. Bruce Forsyth played a bit of piano with us, too, but I've never quite forgotten that when he got up to sing 'The Lady is a Tramp' he made a silly mistake - and then blamed us for it. The show, of course, was live, but instead of doing the professional thing and carrying on, he flapped his hands to stop the music, then turned round and said, "Come on, Ken, get it right this time." Luckily, not many of the guests did things like that.

I remember one show with Frankie Vaughan. He'd brought us the music for the song called 'One' by Marvin Hamlisch from the show *A Chorus Line* and it was really difficult. It still is. I hadn't read music since the Sid Phillips days; John Bennett wasn't a strong reader either and Andy Cooper couldn't read at all. We went to pre-record the backing tape and when it came out it was all right but still a nightmare. As a general rule, though, we could handle stuff; we'd just play whatever song it was by ear and everything was fine. If we did use backing tracks, however - because some of the sequences were filmed outside - we used go and record in another studio in the morning. Anita Harris was one of those who always used backing tracks, I remember.

There's another story - and I've never seen anything like this in my life. This bloke was an escapologist and his act was to put on a straitjacket and tie himself to the branch of a tree just outside the studio. It was about 30ft high, and there he was, dangling from a rope. Then he'd set light to the rope. This, supposedly, gave him about 30 seconds to get himself out of the straitjacket, climb up the burning rope and hang onto the branch of the tree. Well anyway, he didn't make it. The rope burnt through and there was this terrible thud; we honestly thought he was dead. Luckily, his act had been pre-recorded in the afternoon, and when he came on in the evening they actually ran the clip of the disaster on the show - a 'here's one we recorded earlier' type of thing. And then, of course, it was "How're you feeling ...?" "Oh, not too bad - just a broken neck ... and arm ... and ribs and leg ..."!

It was a great time, but in 1981 we were told that *Saturday*

*Night at the Mill* was over, so there we were, back on the road again.

### John's Journal: 18 December 1977, Pebble Mill Studios, Birmingham

*I've just been 'cobwebbed': sprayed with a spun nylon and rubber solution from the Pebble Mill TV special effects department. On the show the nylon strands got wrapped round my trombone slide and glued the thing up! A few weeks ago I was 'snowed'. Polystyrene chips were showered on us during the* Jim'll Fix It *TV show. A similar thing happened: polystyrene got stuck down the brass tubes, eventually blocking the whole thing. Another time the whole band spent about two hours being made up to look as though we were completely bald - apart from banjoist Tony Pitt who was bald anyway and was given a big curly wig. It was all for nothing, as the producer decided he wasn't going to use that effect. I dunno; the things we do for our art!*

# 8
# BEHIND THE IRON CURTAIN

**John:**

*In September 1964 we had our first experience of life behind the old Iron Curtain, when the band undertook a two-week tour of Romania. Word filtered home that our reception there had been sensational - "Like Beatlemania," blared the national press. **Beetle** mania would've been nearer the mark, for as soon as we arrived at our hotel in Bucharest we ran into a plague of enormous bugs, the size and weight of old pennies, which plopped down upon us like a black hail storm. Within seconds we were ankle deep in the things. Some spun on their backs with legs waving feebly; others dived in our beer or slipped down our shirt fronts. What none of the giant insects seemed capable of doing, despite all their lethargic activity, was to get airborne. So it remains a mystery how the swarm had managed to attain sufficient altitude to mount a Kamikaze attack on us in the first place. As the evening drew on we had a bit of fun scooping up armfuls of these crawling insects and tearing around the hotel rooms to deposit mounds of them in each other's beds.*

**Kenny:**

Another time we were at Bucharest doing a concert and had to finish at 11 p.m. to catch the midnight train on to the next city. We had several people with us: a lady interpreter, our own roadie, and two more local men who handled the gear. Anyhow, one of them said, "You go on ahead. Just get on the train and we'll see to the gear." So that was what we did. The drums and bass were loaded onto the train - only just! - after which all the doors were locked from the inside. We didn't know anything about all this, of course, as by then we were in our carriage playing cards and drinking vodka. We found out later that the bloke had then made a desperate leap onto the buffers just as the train set off, and he'd somehow made his way forwards along the outside of the coaches. Suddenly we saw this ghostly white face peering in at us from outside the window! Fortunately, a signalman had seen him hanging onto the train and had sent a warning ahead to stop it. And it was going at some bloody speed, I can tell you. But the point was that this man didn't want to lose his job. The 'authorities' would've had him. When we finally pulled him inside he was as pale as death. We poured some vodka down him and slowly he came back to life. But that was what it was like in the Eastern Bloc back then, before the Berlin Wall came down - Big Brother was always watching you!

### John:

*At one point we began to wonder if the band had blotted its copybook, as our hosts seemed increasingly nervous, not to say suspicious, about what we might be getting up to after hours. One night I drifted into a cellar club to sit in with a local jazz band, only to be collared on stage by a couple of 'bodyguards' and unceremoniously marched out. When I protested about having my arms pinioned behind me all the way back to the hotel, I was politely informed that it was for my own protection. That's funny, I thought - had my trombone playing sounded that grim?*

### Kenny:

Dave Jones liked a drink. Late one night in a Bucharest hotel he staggered into the room I was sharing with him, got undressed, and then took a glance at his reflection in the full-length wardrobe mirror. He mustn't have liked what he saw, because without a word he just smashed his fist into that mirror! There was glass everywhere, and Dave was stumbling around on it in his bare feet. Then he fell flat on his face on the bed and passed out. The next morning it took him half an hour to get the bits of glass out of the soles of his feet, while I made my apologies to the manager for the broken mirror and the blood on the blankets.

**John:**

*Our first tour of East Germany was in September 1966. Those were the days of the Cold War and the Berlin Wall, and East Germany was so cut off that none of us knew what to expect on the other side. But the GDR (German Democratic Republic) always treated British jazz bands well and paid us enough in non-transferable East German marks to allow us to live like kings - while we were there.*

*The Kenny Ball Band made 11 visits to the GDR over a period of 25 years, after which East Germany became just Germany - and in a strange way not quite as interesting. Throughout that quarter of a century there were bound to be bad times as well as good times; though even the worst times were never that bad.*

**Kenny:**

Getting into East Germany that very first time was a spooky experience. Someone had escaped over the Berlin Wall the previous week and everyone was on edge. We were stopped at the frontier and told to drive the van into what looked like a garage. Then we had to get out while the soldiers searched the van, even putting mirrors on long poles underneath to search for I don't know what. Finally, our passports were stamped and we were let through. It'd taken over an hour since they'd first unlocked all our cases and started rooting around inside. Welcome to East Berlin, we thought!

## John's Journal: East Berlin, Wednesday 7 September 1966

*On a raised lookout platform near the Brandenburg Gate, where the broad avenue of the Unter den Linden ends abruptly at the East Berlin frontier, a tiny crowd of Eastern Bloc citizens gathers each day to stare across into West Germany. Out of curiosity I joined them, and spotted far away on the western side a similar, though better-dressed, crowd staring back at us. Unlike my companions, who seemed gloomily engrossed in gazing at their mirror image, this didn't strike me as an ideal way to spend the rest of the afternoon, so I moved off and headed east.*

*I kept going until I glimpsed something white at the far end of a street. Making towards it, I suddenly found myself face-to-face with a remote stretch of the Berlin Wall: an unbroken panorama of concrete that swept away into infinity on either side. Jerry-built, I would say, in every sense of the term. In the shadow of the Wall stood a group of border guards. It seemed a perfect opportunity, so I switched the lens of my cine camera to telephoto, lined them up in the viewfinder, and sprayed them with a brief automatic burst of 8mm film - bang, bang, bang, you're all dead!*

*Well, three of them would've been. The fourth guard already had his binoculars trained on me, and during the fleeting moment that we were simultaneously tele-focused on each other it crossed my mind that this was not such a good idea after all. There followed an alarming cacophony of shouts, the stamping of rifle butts on concrete, and gestures for me to come forward and explain myself.*

*Without pause for thought I leapt to one side with amazing agility and collided with a party of Cuban tourists, who'd been contentedly studying their guidebooks until I took them all out like a well-aimed ten-pin bowling ball. While the dust was settling I peered through the jumble of arms and legs and grabbed my chance; haring round the nearest corner and zig-zagging off into the sunset like the end of a Tom and Jerry cartoon. This is getting silly; I'm tired of muck and bullets; it's about time I stopped believing I'm taking part in a Len Deighton spy movie!*

**Kenny:**

Our second tour of East Germany was in 1968, when we recorded a live concert at the Friedrichstadt Palast, a massive building, with thousands of young fans going wild over us. Even now it stands out as the best live concert we've ever recorded.

In the second half I said, "We'll do 'Ain't Misbehavin'." The place went mad. Over the noise I heard someone call, "Bravo, Kenny! One more time!" He's on the record, sounding like Count Basie with a German accent.

**John:**

*The recording tapes were played back to us the following morning in a mansion that had once belonged to Hermann Goering. The house was situated right on the border between East and West Berlin, and when we arrived we were taken into the cellars and proudly shown the entrance to an underground tunnel that leads under the River Spree into the west - or used to, before it was blocked up with concrete.*

*Upstairs we sat listening to the tapes while gazing out the window at the West Berlin government building across the water, which was proudly flying the West German flag. The sound engineer had done such an excellent job that we gave him a round of applause. Then, while decisions were being made as to which numbers were to be included on the prospective album, Vic Pitt, Andy Cooper and myself strolled outside for a breath of fresh air. We crossed the courtyard, went through the gates and leaned over the railing on the other side of the alley. Below us swirled the murky waters of the River Spree, with all its submarine nets and mines hidden in its depths, and on the far bank lay West Berlin. Unlike the citizens of the GDR, we were free to go there whenever we wished, but, to give him his due, the armed soldier who had quietly stolen up behind us wouldn't have known that.*

"*Gotterdammerung!*" *he yelled, or words to that effect. Startled, we turned and regarded him blankly. The soldier then addressed us with a long stream of what sounded like guttural swearing. Vic Pitt shrugged his shoulders. "Dunno what you're on about, cocky," he said. The soldier's eyes narrowed. He hadn't understood what Vic was saying, but he didn't like his tone. He unslung his weapon, grabbed Vic by his coat collar and dragged him back across the alley. With one hand on the nape of Vic's neck, he made him read the red and white notice that warns trespassers of the consequences of straying too near the frontier. Then he moved away, folded his arms and regarded the three of us with suspicion.*

*We noticed that he was wearing a cheap civilian shirt under his tunic, had two-day stubble on his chin, and his breath smelt of stale garlic. He wasn't interested in anything we had to say.*

*Fortunately, the woman caretaker of the recording studio made a timely appearance at the gateway of Goering's one-time residence and frantically beckoned us. "You must come here now!" she called. We walked towards her, trying not to look as though we were in too much of a hurry, as the guard was stalking us only a few paces behind. It seemed a longer walk back to the gate, mainly because the guard was pinging some gadget on his automatic rifle that made it sound as though he were trying to get a tune out of it. "The taxi comes soon into the courtyard," explained the woman nervously when we reached the gate. "You must not be outside the courtyard until you are in the taxi." It sounded like extremely sensible advice at the time.*

*Our album was issued in East Germany the following year. It was a great success and a second volume was released there in 1980, both of which continued to sell well behind the Iron Curtain for several more years. In 1969 some of the numbers from that East Berlin concert were re-issued in the UK as an album on the Fontana label. By then our first East Berlin concert album had reached the number two spot on the shortlist of best-sellers of all time in East Germany. But still at number one, we were informed, was an album of Hitler's wartime speeches. If, as John Lennon once notoriously claimed, The Beatles are more popular*

*than Jesus Christ, then it can also be said of the Kenny Ball Jazzmen*
*that they are almost as popular as Der Fuehrer.*

**Kenny:**

Leipzig was a historic and interesting city. Our concert there
went down very well - the audience shouting for encore upon
encore, stomping their feet like tom-toms and throwing sprays
of flowers on stage. A couple of hours later we were in the
Midnight Bar of the hotel, buying champagne by the bucketful
and paying with handfuls of Monopoly money, which had to be
squandered there in East Germany as it was totally worthless
anywhere else in the world.

### John's Journal: Leipzig, September 1968

*Another great concert tonight, during which we were kept well*
*lubricated by a local brew thoughtfully supplied by the management.*
*By the end of the show I was so well lubricated I had hiccups, and*
*having stupidly decided to walk back alone to our hotel I soon had*
*no idea where I was. Fifteen minutes later I stumbled into the main*
*railway station.*
*At this time of night the station was almost deserted apart from a*
*group of young East German soldiers, who were passing the time*
*waiting for their train by practising their goose-stepping drill. I*
*happened to be lurching past them, minding my own business, when,*
*due to a sudden lack of concentration, I lapsed into an involuntary*
*soft-shoe shuffle, which sent me off on a tangent sideways. It did*
*briefly enter my mind that these clockwork soldiers might think I was*
*taking the piss out of them with my boozy Fred Astaire routine, but*
*by then I was completely out of control. And out of their sight,*
*fortunately, for the momentum had whisked me laterally through the*
*open doors of a stationary railway carriage and out the open doors*
*on the opposite side. Having unintentionally made my exit stage*

*right, I now found myself on a different platform, and anxious that no one else should catch sight of my antics I pulled myself together, took a deep breath, glanced importantly at my watch, and tottered off briskly for the exit.*

*The time by my watch was either five past six or twelve thirty-five, depending on whether in my confusion I'd strapped it on upside down or was just not focusing properly. Either way, it felt long past my bedtime. The street outside looked a mile wide, but on the far side, wonder of wonders, I could actually see my ̇destination, the neon sign of the Stadt-Leipzig hotel. I started off across the shining cobweb of tramlines, so intent on keeping the giant façade of the hotel directly ahead of me that I failed to notice the group of elderly road-sweepers in my path. The collision caused brooms to fly and trolleys to career off down the tramlines at all angles. Mumbling my apologies, I benevolently handed each man a crisp and valueless ten-mark note, which they accepted in utter bafflement!*

*I stumbled up to the fourth floor and paused outside my room. At that moment my nerve endings were telling me - as no doubt James Bond's nerve endings would have told him under similar circumstances - that all was not well. I opened the door cautiously, my steely gaze flickered round the darkened room, and I stepped forward into three inches of water. I should mention that East German hotel plumbing is one of this country's major hazards. My lavatory cistern must have begun overflowing the moment I'd left the room several hours earlier, and had been overflowing ever since.*

*To reach the cistern I climbed on the toilet seat - which was a mistake, as the rusting hinges gave way under my weight. Fortunately, I fell into the bath, which was the only dry place in the room. Standing on the rim of the bath I could just about reach into the cistern. I located the ballcock by touch and was able to bend it slightly. Just enough, in fact, to snap the corroded thing off. I climbed down and stood in shallow water, balancing the broken-off orb of the ballcock in one hand. I remained in this position for a while, deep in thought, like*

*King Canute clutching his regalia while facing the incoming tide. It was getting late, I was plastered, and decisions had to be made. The decision I made was to shut the door on the chaos in the bathroom and go to bed. After testing the bed gingerly in case it was rigged to collapse like everything else in this blasted country, I took one final hefty swig of vodka and clambered in.*

### Kenny:

One time in East Germany we were passing through what looked just like a picturesque Olde English village, complete with green and duck pond, when my Jag ran out of petrol. We called in at the local pub, and the innkeeper seemed a jovial chap. When he realised that we needed assistance he dashed outside and stopped a passing policeman on a motorbike. This policeman looked quite dangerous; he was dressed in leather, with a gun on his belt, and he stared at us for a long time through the dark lenses of his goggles before he and his bike roared off down the track in a cloud of greasy black fumes.

After he'd gone we ordered beer and sausages all round. Then some time later there was a noise of backfiring, and the policeman came in the doorway carrying a full can of petrol, which he presented to us, gratis. We invited him to join us for a beer or two and the atmosphere began to get jolly. We could've made a night of it if we hadn't a gig to go to. When we finally arrived at Reisa an hour late, the entire concert audience was standing in the street outside the stage door. As our two vehicles approached, the crowd whooped and cheered like they were greeting a liberating army. The theatre manager was so relieved to see us that he presented us with a full crate of beer.

### John's Journal: East Berlin

### 14 March 1974

*Ron Bowden and I are sharing a hotel room. The phone rang this*

114

*morning to wake us for the group shopping spree in downtown
Berlin, and as Ron reached out for the receiver his bed collapsed in
a cloud of dust. Ron was not at all amused when I fell about
laughing. Still chortling, I left Ron in the remains of his bed and
went to the tiny loo, where in no time at all I somehow contrived to
get my foot trapped in between the lavatory bowl and the door. It took
me ten minutes to extricate myself. To give him his due, Ron didn't
guffaw.*

*Later this morning I went back to the hotel to find our banjo/guitar
player Ted Baldwin in the coffee shop, sitting glumly beside an
enormous Wagnerian maiden with flaxen hair. Last night Ted had
chatted up the prettier dark-haired sister of this lady and had invited
her up to his room. She told him that he should go upstairs first and
turn out all the lights. She would follow a few moments later - the
idea being to throw the STASI secret police off the scent. Soon
afterwards there came a discreet knock at Ted's door and in the
darkness he let the girl in. They thrashed around for a few moments,
during which Ted began to sense that things weren't quite as they
should be. He switched on the light and found he had been making
hay with the gigantic flaxen-haired one. She was his for the night,
and threatened to scream if he asked her to leave.*

### 15 March

*Yesterday, in Dresden, our pianist Johnny Parker entered a vast
ornate building believing it to be the Central Art Gallery. Instead he
found he had blundered into an exhibition of the public transport
system of Budapest. Although not a great fan of Hungarian trams,
John nevertheless felt he ought to feign some interest as he seemed to
be the only visitor that day - or any other, come to that - and had
already shaken the aged curator out of a coma in order to pay him
his one mark entrance fee. So he spent a miserable half-hour
squeaking around the deserted building in his new East German
shoes, staring bleakly at gigantic transformers and dynamos.*

*Although the curator didn't volunteer any information on the exhibits, he persisted in following John around from gallery to gallery, and by a strange coincidence he too had squeaky shoes and a pronounced limp similar to John's. Their squeak-bump, squeak-bump duet was so perfectly matched in tempo that at one point John turned to his shadow and enquired politely: "Are you taking the piss?"*

### 16 March

*The coach left the autobahn and wound through hilly countryside, everyone craning their necks hoping to be the first to spot the famous castle.*

*A bend in the road, a wide stretch of river ahead, and suddenly on the opposite bank loomed the title scene from the film 'The Colditz Story': an escarpment with a massive grey stone fortress perched on its summit. The coach crossed a bridge, climbed a steeply curving driveway, passed through two arched gateways and finally drew up in the cobbled courtyard.*

*We alighted and gazed up at the irregular rows of small barred windows. The place looked deserted. The shutter of one window was flapping in the breeze. Now and then small pieces of crumbling masonry fell on the cobbles below.*

*We would have liked to have investigated further, but the administrator explained that it would not be safe for us to roam around inside the castle - especially upstairs. It was not just the fact that Colditz Castle is currently a mental asylum. Apparently the main building was in danger of collapse. Owing to the many tons of earth that had been transported out of various wartime escape tunnels and hidden away among the rafters in the attics, the castle was now top-heavy and its foundations weak. That was the administrator's excuse anyway, and we left Colditz Castle without having seen any sign of its current inmates - the 300 psychiatric patients who have been committed here. Apart, that is, from one cadaverous face that peered down at us from an upper window as we were leaving. John Parker waved cheerily to the apparition and muttered: "God rest ye Jerry mental men."*

### 4 November

*A TV show in Leipzig. Accidents continue to follow me around. Today, while rehearsing my trombone solo on 'Avalon', I must have inadvertently cast the evil eye on a TV cameraman homing in on me for a close-up. He had been cruising sedately towards me along a raised plinth when for no apparent reason he lost control of his machine. I lowered the trombone bell and watched in stunned silence as technician and camera toppled sideways in slow motion. A fraction of a second later there came a splintering crunch of metal on concrete. RIP camera!*

*And cameraman presumably. After the accident he turned pale and dropped to a crouch, holding his head in his hands. He wasn't hurt, but he looked as shattered as his camera. Press photographers leapt forwards to record the tragic scene - as evidence for the subsequent trial, perhaps?*

### 5 November

*I was relieved to see the unfortunate TV cameraman back in action at the studio today - in charge of a brand-new camera. "Is better," he told us proudly, "because is American-made." He was grateful for our sympathy, but he would prefer to forget what happened yesterday. I don't blame him; so would I. And for his own well-being I would suggest he leaves off praising American technology!*

*We are accompanied on this trip by Colin Hogg, our agent. Colin thinks East Germany is a hilarious country, and spends much of his time chuckling over the absurdities of life here. When Colin Hogg chuckles he has to poke his tongue out in order to keep his false teeth roughly in position. Not a pretty sight. It got worse when, as the evening wore on, he went a bit Jekyll-and-Hyde; transforming himself from a fairly average-looking British businessman into a little fat drunken vandal. Hogg into pig, as it were. One of his antics was to traipse around outside the hotel doing Hitler impressions while goose-stepping through a flower bed. He laughed so much he nearly lost his false teeth among the antirrhinums. Hogg collects antiques, Meissen porcelain in particular, and his sole reason for being here with us is to try and con some little old East German ladies out of their treasured keepsakes.*

**Kenny:**

We came off stage after one concert, got changed and waited in the dressing room while the gear was being packed away. All of a sudden there was a kind of explosion - the washbasin that our banjoist and guitar player Tony Pitt had been leaning against had come away from the wall! Two jets of water shot out and everyone started yelling and running around in circles. The water level in the dressing room rose to about four inches and then we began to see the funny side. As the stream flowed out of the door and down the passage a figure darted in, turned off the mains tap and just vanished. We never did find out who he was.

### John's Journal: 1978 Tour of East Germany

#### 17 February

*Last night's concert was held in the main hall of the Trade's Union College. The front row was occupied by stony-faced party members, who sat rigidly with their arms folded. They all wore, as Ken put it, make-me-laugh expressions. Behind them sat row upon row of students, all determined not to put a foot wrong or show themselves up. It was not an ideal formula for a successful jazz concert. From the start we knew that the entire audience would be taking its cue from the centre of the front row. If Herr Direktor decided to applaud,* so would they. If not, there would be a nasty silence. "We'll just have to play to ourselves and do a Hallo Folks," said Ken, which when decoded translates as 'if the worst comes to the worst let's all pretend we're having a good time up here on stage.' That's easier said than done. What with one thing and another there was a bit of a constrained atmosphere throughout the first half.

A life-sized bust of Karl Marx stood at stage left, dangerously close to Andy Cooper. At interval time, as we were leaving the stage, Andy reached out, gave the statue a friendly pat on its head, and remarked, "See you soon, Charlie."

There was a brief shocked silence, after which a deep rumble started to erupt somewhere in the front row, and developed into a throaty chuckle. It spread along the row as some of the big-cheese hard-liners rose from their seats to applaud. This in turn released a tidal wave of cheering from the rows immediately behind, and almost instantaneously the floodgates were opened up - the kids to the rear began roaring and cackling hysterically until tears were rolling down their faces. Even when we reached our dressing room a floor below we could still hear faint laughter coming from the auditorium. It was as though an escape valve had released all that community repression in one blast. Ken didn't see it like that; he seemed rather bemused by the reaction. "I didn't think it was all that funny," he said.

### John's Journal: Leipzig

### 18 February 1978

Our bass player John Benson's new nickname is 'Animal'. He has been revealed as the phantom figure who sidles around bars after hours biting men's bums at random. Strange but true. Recently, Tony Pitt and Andy Cooper refined this curious practice into what they call the 'stereo version', in which they approach a person from opposite sides then bite in unison. John Benson, who started all this nonsense, was appropriately the first to be subjected to a stereo attack

*in a flurry of arms and legs. It was like a riot in a dog pound.*
*Benson's teeth are very white and canine. Tonight in the hotel bar the*
*sound of his voice steadily gained in volume as it so often does.*
*People sitting at a long table nearby lost the thread of their*
*conversations. Heads turned. Munching a salami roll, Benson*
*glared at them and roared: "What are you lot all looking at?"*
*Moments later he was crawling under their table to the far end,*
*where he bit an East German drummer on the leg.*

### 19 February

*A peculiar incident occurred tonight on stage. Halfway through his*
*speech to the audience at the beginning of the first half, Karlheinz*
*Drechsel suddenly leapt sideways in the direction of Animal Benson;*
*his aim apparently being to catch Benson off guard and bite him in*
*the neck. This kind of mayhem is definitely not Karlheinz's scene; at*
*the very least he should have rehearsed it. The outcome was that the*
*bite missed its mark and Karlheinz scampered away giggling in*
*embarrassment, only to slip and fall flat on his back in the wings.*
*God knows what the audience made of it - here was their eminent*
*middle-aged broadcaster transformed before their eyes into*
*Christopher Lee playing a guest role in Carry On Screaming.*
*After the interval Karlheinz sheepishly came back on stage to make*
*his customary second half announcement, unaware that Andy*
*Cooper was right behind him, loping along on all fours like a great*
*hairy wolfhound. Andy sunk his teeth into Karlheinz's leg;*
*Karlheinz squealed and darted away, only to be intercepted by*
*Animal Benson and Tony Pitt, who hefted him up and carried him*
*backstage, giggling like a schoolgirl. It's odd that everyone who has*
*received tooth marks on this tour has then turned into an attacker*
*himself. Perhaps there really is something in that old vampire legend*
*after all. The 'bit biter', to coin a phrase.*
*Benson's antics even attracted the attention of the paparazzi, hence*
*the item in the William Hickey column of the Daily Express, of*

*February 1978:*

*"Are jazzmen turning to the revolting ways of punk rockers? At an East German diplomatic dinner Kenny Ball's bass-expert, John 'Animal' Benson, suddenly slid under the table, crawled along and bit clarinettist colleague Andy Cooper on the leg. Moments later Cooper was under the table too, crawling back to gnash Benson on the hand so hard that it bled. This behaviour is apparently quite common. Cooper even bit an East German promoter on the leg in Leipzig in front of 3000 people."*

### 20 February

*The state-owned Mitropa restaurant we stopped at today on the autobahn offered the customary menu: goulash with pickled swedes and boiled potatoes. I overheard John Parker telling Karlheinz Drechsel: "In England there are several varieties of potatoes."*

*"Here there is only one variety," replied Karlheinz despondently.*

*"Yes, well of course there would be," said John. "Ours are mostly bourgeois potatoes, of course. But we do also have socialist potatoes, working class potatoes, proletariat potatoes ..." At which point I closed my ears; I'd heard enough.*

*I had a piece of cake for afters. It didn't look much but tasted nice and brought back memories of childhood. That's because it was baked with powdered eggs and soya flour like the utility stuff we used to eat in wartime.*

*Later, at the hotel I entered the lift, pressed the Down button and typically the lift shot up to the seventh floor. The doors slid open and there stood guitarist Tony Pitt in his Groucho mask, blasting away on some peculiar musical instrument - an assortment of motor horns and trumpet valves haphazardly soldered together - as though he was setting off for a New Year's Eve party. After having scared to death the rush-hour passengers on a Dresden tram with it, Tony now intends to take the thing home, hang it on his wall and fill it with*

121

*flowers. Rather an anticlimax I'd say ...*

*We reached Berlin at midday and I strode out into the icy wind to Marx-Engels Platz, where I bought a handbag and two alarm clocks, one of which does not work. I then queued up in a supermarket for a loaf and a packet of spam. Then back to my hotel room, where I brewed peppermint tea using my gadget for boiling water, which I stirred with the nail file out of my handbag. This sort of behaviour is what passes for self-sufficiency in the latter days of a tour in East Germany.*

### 21 February

*This morning I bought myself a loaf of rye bread, some cheese and a slab of butter. I decided on my spartan lunch menu today after deftly catching a Spanish onion, which Ken had magnanimously tossed over his shoulder for the hungry peasants in the rear of the coach.*

*That's the trouble with East German tours: from affluence at the start, one is reduced to penury by the end. East German marks are plentiful but non-transferable, so you feel obliged to spend the lot while you are here. The problem is getting the timing right. But you can always cheer yourself up in the knowledge that the poorer you are, the closer you must be to going home.*

*After the concert tonight a grim-faced policeman entered our dressing room and stood watching us in silence as we wrapped ourselves up in our winter woollies for the long overnight drive ahead. At last he spoke - in English. "Many people have been killed tonight," he said darkly. We backed against the walls. Were we that bad? Was this to be another night of the long knives? But the policeman had only come in to warn us about the dangers of travelling by night on the icy roads. "Drive carefully," he called as we left.*

### Kenny:

Travelling back through East Germany to get to West Berlin you have to pass through the Helmstedt frontier. The traffic slows to slow to a crawl. Which on one occasion gave us time to watch a sergeant and four privates playing cricket using an empty beer crate as their wicket outside the British army's NAAFI building. The Union Jack was fluttering on a flagpole nearby. Jolly good show, chaps.

### John's Journal: East Germany

#### 28 January 1988

*Cobblestones; coal smoke; trams; and members of the Kenny Ball band scampering around carrying brand-new suitcases - a fairly typical scene at the midpoint of an East German tour when everyone is still fairly solvent. The idea is to spend a spare morning filling one's empty suitcase with useful things. We never learn. Ron Weatherburn used to have the right idea. He always sought out the monstrously silly; a zither, a bow and arrow, a stethoscope, even a single ski! Bandleader Alan Elsdon also had a brilliant idea with his East German variation on the game of Monopoly, where one starts as a millionaire and the aim is get rid of all one's money. The winner is the first to declare himself a beggar.*

*The concert took place in the Weimarhalle - previously known as the Hermann Goering Halle. After it was over I spotted a very polite German speaking to Andy.*

*"Good afternoon," said the man as he left.*

*"Good morning," replied Andy. As it was 11 o'clock at night when this exchange took place, it struck me as quaintly funny - like a punchline from ITMA in 1943.*

#### 2 February

*This morning I descended in the lift alongside the captain of the British Military Mission stationed in Potsdam. He knew all about the band's regular tours of East Germany (well he would, wouldn't he?)*

*"I spotted your signatures in the visitors book at Colditz Castle," he said brightly, adding with a smile, "I may drop in on your concert when you play Potsdam." Surely not to check whether we're passing over any state secrets!*

**Kenny:**

When we first came to East Germany back in 1966, no one would've placed bets on the Berlin Wall being toppled before the end of the next millennium, let alone the current one. Germany's unification in 1989 took everyone by surprise; us especially, as our eleventh trip had been negotiated during the final days of Communist rule. When we arrived there in 1991 it felt strange to be greeted by old friends amid familiar surroundings, but in a completely different country.

### John's Journal: 19 March 1991

*East Germany is now West Germany - or just Germany I suppose. Ron Bowden was complaining that he'd just paid a woman 20 pfennigs for a visit to the loo. We reminisced about the old days when we would have given her 100 East German marks for the same privilege. "That one's probably retired by now," mused Ron. "She'd have earned enough to buy her own shithouse."*

**Kenny:**

In October 1984 we did the first tour by a British band in Communist Russia. Other bands, including Benny Goodman, had been there, but we were the first band to travel all around the country. And we were also asked to play the 'Presidium' actually inside the Kremlin. This was just before Gorbachev was elected, and they asked us to play 'Midnight in Moscow', which we did. And funnily enough, when Gorbachev became Prime

Minister and met Ronald Reagan, they sat at the piano and played a duet of 'Midnight in Moscow' - our version! So we can say we were responsible for détente in some small way!

### John:

*Awaiting us in the terminal building when we first arrived in Russia were our hosts, Igor and Natasha. Igor and Natasha; names that ring like the sleigh bells in* Dr Zhivago. *Both were young: Igor, narrow-eyed and faintly distrustful, had the look of our man from the KGB; while Natasha, in contrast, gave us a sweet, welcoming smile. First appearances can be deceptive; later we discovered that Natasha was the boss of this enterprise and that underneath those pretty ballerina features lurked a heart of pure cast iron. Natasha spoke perfect English, while Igor almost spoke English. It's a difference of degree, but Igor's efforts to find the correct English grammar made us laugh; so within a day or two he was accepted as one of the lads.*

### Kenny:

Before we came to Russia we decided to get some t-shirts made with 'Kenny Ball and his Jazzmen' in Russian gold lettering across the front. We wore them on most of the concerts there and had great fun. But towards the end of the tour we were in Leningrad, and an English-speaking Russian said to me, "I love your t-shirts."

I said proudly, "Yes, we had them specially made to say 'Kenny Ball and his Jazzmen'."

"Oh no," he chuckled, "it says 'Kenny Ball and HER Jazzmen'."!

### John:

*Our month's tour of Russia went down a storm, but there was one sticky moment right at the start, when our banjo/guitarist John Fenner became so anxious about conditions in the Soviet Union he told us he would rather leave the band than stay one moment longer!*

*Our hosts might've taken this as an insult, and everyone tried their utmost to make Fenner change his mind. The talking went on throughout the night, but he was adamant: he wanted to go home and that was that. The following morning, as we prepared to board the coach for our first gig in Russia, we lined up to shake hands with Fenner, who bade each of us a clipped farewell as though he was captain of the Titanic and we were claiming the last remaining lifeboat. The coach then drew away. Nobody looked back. "End of an era," someone muttered; it might've been me. John Benson then drew our attention to the fact that Fenner had told us he was going to leave Moscow at midnight last night. Midnight in Moscow! That seemed quite important to us at the time - the stuff of which legends are made.*

*Much later we heard the story of John Fenner's final hours in Russia from his own lips. Apparently he'd visited the British Embassy, where he was told, "No problem. Just get yourself to the Aeroflot office and get your ticket."*

*Fenner called a taxi. "Take me to the Aeroflot office," he demanded. "Quick as you can."*

*"I want to buy your watch," replied the taxi driver solemnly.*

*It was, Fenner said, not an auspicious start. Eventually, he was deposited outside a large building.*

*"I would like to purchase a ticket to London," he said meekly to the person behind the desk, who could speak English fairly well but seemed nonplussed with Fenner's request.*

*"There are no buses going to London today," he said.*

*"I don't want a bus! Why would I want a bus? I want a plane!" exclaimed Fenner, frantically flapping his arms to illustrate.*

*"Then you must go to the building next door - this is Moscow Bus Station."*

**Kenny:**

We bought Igor, our Russian road manager, a watch for his

birthday. I think we were allowed 50 roubles a day each, and that's like £50, to spend just on food and drink. Anyway, we all clubbed together and we bought a 200-rouble watch for him. He was over the moon, and he cried. He was very nice; I found him a pleasant chap. Perhaps he was a secret agent, but very, very clever, and a very gifted linguist, too. He spoke good English - like what I do!

### John:

*On the night of Igor's birthday we'd arranged to take our Russian hosts for a top-class meal. In the restaurant the wine was soon flowing freely, and at one point I noticed Igor had got up to dance. He was dancing by himself - a kind of slow jig involving a fluttering handkerchief. It looked rather elegant, and people at a nearby table stopped eating and drinking for a moment to applaud him when the music ended. As midnight approached, Andy presented Igor with his new watch. Everyone sang 'Happy Birthday' to Igor, who was now 28 years old. He was overwhelmed, and tears ran down his cheeks. He attempted a speech of thanks, but all he could manage was a tearful, "Hip, hip, hooray, English people." Igor went round the table, clasping our hands in both of his. He now had a watch on each wrist. He'd worn his other watch for the past 14 years: a present from his parents for passing his school exams.*

*Much later the Lithuanian band's mournful melodies were being drowned out by some hearty British vocalising. "It's the same the whole world over," roared Tony Pitt. "It's the rich what gets the blame. It's the poor what gets the pleasure …" (Tony had purposely inverted the lyrics to suit the prevailing political climate.) 'Daisy, Daisy'; 'Tipperary'; our patriotic sentiments were not lost on the party at the table next to us, who competed with a selection of their own native Lithuanian folk songs.*

*Much, much, much later we became aware that the restaurant was about to close, as an apologetic doorman had been plucking at our sleeves.*

*"Tell him to piss off," said Andy to Igor.*

"Okay, okay," replied Igor, and with a silly grin he said to the doorman, "Excuse me, sir. Will you please piss off?"

Ron Bowden had lost his glasses; Steve the roadie had broken his. Pianist Martin Litton, with his trilby tilted forward over his face, was being carried over the cobblestones by Andy and Tony. Igor's birthday was over for another year.

### Kenny:

He was a funny chap, Igor. Know what he said when I asked him if he'd read the Bible? "I haf not read it, but I think I know ze plot!"

### John:

I remember on one of our coach journeys Ken tried to teach Igor cockney rhyming slang. Igor, in serious mode, was trying his hardest to master the niceties. "Mince pies - eyes," he was murmuring solemnly. "Yes, yes, I think now I understand."

In return, when we arrived at the next gig Igor tried to teach Ken how to do the Soviet military goose-step. Igor (who, of course, had been trained to do it properly) demonstrated the correct drill: leg stretched out straight; toes pointed forward; arm brought across the midriff; fierce expression … Igor did it immaculately. Not so Ken. He tried his best, but on the strength of his goose-stepping performance he wouldn't have got the gig with the Hitler Youth let alone the Soviet army!

### Kenny:

We played in Kaunas in Lithuania, and it was the filthiest place I'd ever seen in my life. We played 'Midnight in Moscow' there and it got booed. I thought, that's a good start. We were staying at a hotel in Vilnius, the capital of Lithuania. While there, we were shadowed all the time by - well - I suppose it must've been the KGB. Anyway, Pete Brown, our roadie, had teamed up with a lovely lady who was the Lithuanian tour representative there.

She was very tall, blonde, and spoke German, which meant that Pete Brown and I could communicate with her. Pete really took a fancy to her. So he asked me if he could swap his bedroom, which was quite small, for mine, which was a huge suite. We knew the hotel rooms were bugged, but all I wanted was somewhere to lay my head down, so that didn't bother me. We also knew that Pete had a night of fun, because we could hear it all down the bloody corridor. I've always wondered whether the 'authorities' manning the bugging devices thought it was me making oompah with the Lithuanian German-speaking person!

### John's Journal: Lithuania

#### 15 October 1984

*The exterior of the venue at Kaunas looked to have been designed by an devotee of ancient ruins. Its rear entrance gaped into darkness and was about as inviting as the gateway to a ransacked tomb. We traipsed in silence along wet-flagstoned corridoors that sloped down towards the vast backstage area. There we halted. A faint reek of garlic hung on the air and the only sound was a delicate tapping, which at first I took to be either the drip of slime off damp walls, or the patter of rodent feet.*

*In fact, the tapping sounds came from on stage, where in a spotlit circle two workmen were frantically trying to hammer the disassembled parts of a grand piano back into its shell. Such supreme effort put me in mind of a naval gun team rehearsing for the Royal Tournament.  From where we stood their task looked hopeless - there were more than enough parts strewn around the stage to rebuild three grand pianos. The scene, framed in the glare of that giant spotlight, was reminiscent of an old Laurel and Hardy two-reeler in which another fine mess was being made of a model-T Ford.*

*We dumped our bags in a changing room that may once have stabled Peter The Great's third-best horses. There we stood awhile, staring into space; everyone deep in their own thoughts.*

*"The nicest thing that's happened to me recently," mused Tony Pitt, "was Tamara [the attractive Russian anouncer] giving me that brittle look and saying, "Tony! Giff me cigarette!"*

*" Wow!" I said. "Here - take two - take the packet - take me! It's those black button eyes, man." Tony shook his head and grinned. "Never knew I had it in me."*

*In the silence that followed, John Benson studied Tony thoughtfully. "And I always thought Monty Sunshine was weird," he said. "He liked slapping pigs' buttocks."*

*"Weird?" said Tony. "What about wossname - that piano player with one eye and one hand? He kept the gig because he had a good ear. Ha ha ha."*

*We changed into our band uniforms, hopping about on damp flagstones to discard our trousers - pianist Martin Litton revealing a voluminous pair of pink shorts from which his legs projected like a pair of pipe cleaners. Andy, with a frown, observed Martin's trouser-dance closely. "Are we doing our Stanley Matthews act tonight?" he enquired, slowly moving in.*

*Realising his predicament, Martin yelped and quickly grabbed the trousers to his band uniform.*

*"You're not going to put trousers on as well?" said Andy in mock disbelief.*

*Martin took off at a run, closely pursued by Andy, whooping. They circled the room a couple of times and eventually reached stalemate either side of a table.*

*"When I joined this band," said Martin breathlessly, "no one told me buggering was in the contract."*

*"You were buggered as soon as you joined," replied Andy.*

*I strode out in search of a loo. I discovered a vestibule backstage that apparently accomodated ladies, gents, and any stray herd of dairy cattle that happened to be taken short in the vicinity. It had no door, no toilet paper, and no toilet. But there was no mistaking what it was used for. I backed away and came up for air, following the meandering passage up to the stage entrance. Dusk had given way to night. Across the street a queue had gathered; apparently an electrical store had just received a fresh consignment of chromium-plated samovars and no one wanted to miss the excitement.*

*I returned by way of the stage. The two Lithuanian workers, I noticed, were looking confident and fairly cheerful - the piano was beginning to take shape. It would be ready, they said, in time for our concert. It was then 6.30 p.m.*

*But it was all right on the night, as they say. When the band went on stage the audience in Kaunas gymnasium erupted in pandemonium.*

*The spotlights dazzle; at first it is hard to focus. The stage is thickly carpeted, the loose boards beneath turning it into a minefield. Step on the end of one board and the other end springs up. Have to be careful; there's nothing more catastrophic for one's dignity than falling arse over elbow in front of 3,000 people. I stubbed my toe. "Oops," I said, grinning foolishly, and from then on I was more cautious; creeping around the stage, legs bent, like Groucho. John Benson gave me a sidelong expressionless glance; I gave him my sickly grin in return. "Got a tangle in your Y-fronts?" he muttered.*

*The show was an emotional experience. By the end of it we were again standing knee-deep in flowers. As the audience rose and swayed to 'All You Need Is Love', just for a moment the world seemed a better place.*

### Kenny:

I remember the last night in Vilnius standing on the station platform waiting for our train to Leningrad. Suddenly there was a commotion, and an old woman came running towards us, flapping her hands. Apparently there was a fire on a train in a siding just beyond the end of the platform. About half a dozen men brought a fire hose from somewhere and carried it in

131

single file across the rails. But the hose turned out to be too short to reach the fire. More hoses were unravelled, but none of these was long enough either. So now there were about a dozen hoses lying across the tracks like white ribbons, all of them dribbling water onto the earth. Then one man brought a bucket, filled it from the nozzle of a hose, and took it to the burning coach in the siding. A couple of moments later back he came, refilled the bucket and went off again to the fire. Meanwhile, the carriages went on burning and none of his workmates bothered to help; they just stood around looking on.

Then our train arrived. Everyone watched as it ran over the fire hoses, chopping them up like live eels! We got on the train and set off for Leningrad, going slowly past the group of firefighters standing stock still amongst the chopped-up bits of hose on the tracks while smoke drifted across from the now blazing coaches in the siding. What a sad memory of our last hour in Vilnius!

# 9
# ROUND THE WORLD

***John:***

*In 1962 Pye chief, Louis Benjamin, returned from Japan with a number he felt might suit the band's style. The song, recorded by Japanese vocalist Kyu Sakamoto had been a big hit in Japan. It also had an unpronounceable title that literally translates as 'I Shall Walk Looking Up'. The lyrics tell of a man who, while walking, looks up and whistles so that his tears won't fall -which, all things considered, didn't bode too well as hit material for the Ball band!*

*However, when given the 'Moscow' treatment and rechristened 'Sukiyaki' (actually the name of a Japanese hotpot dish!), it took off and became our ninth successive entry into the pop charts. This was a real feather in our caps, as The Beatles had then only just emerged as the greatest thing in the pop world since sliced bread.*

*Our 'Sukiyaki' also became a hit around the world - even in Japan, the country of its origin. This led to the band touring there in 1964. I remember the band attending a press conference in Tokyo soon after our arrival. Unshaven and still jet-lagged, we shuffled in single file into a conference room, where we sat at a long table under the solemn gaze of dozens of earnest Japanese faces. The situation reminded me of those grainy newsreels of the 1940s, showing a group of perplexed British army officers being interrogated after the fall of Singapore.*

*It was a bit like an interrogation. One journalist started the ball rolling by acidly reminding us that Kyu Sakamoto's version of 'Ue o Muite Arukō' (to give 'Sukiyaki' its original Japanese title) had topped the Japanese charts long before ours. Another wanted to know why the song had been rechristened 'Sukiyaki': "It is a love song, which has nothing to do with food."*

*There was no answer to that, so we didn't provide one. But the dispute over the new title raged for a while - even as far abroad as the USA, when in the next edition of Newsweek a columnist noted that re-titling Kyu Sakamoto's song was "like issuing 'Moon River' in Japan under the title' Beef Stew'"!*

### Kenny:

We had our first sukiyaki meal on that 1964 tour. At the eating house we took off our shoes at the door and went into a tiny room that had only one table about 12 inches high. There were no chairs; you had to sit cross-legged on the floor. Sitting like that, even for five minutes, is not easy to say the least - we Westerners aren't built the same way as Asians! The hostesses came in with plates of lettuce, mushrooms, bamboo shoots, spring onions and raw, thinly sliced Kobe beef. The Kobe bulls are given beer to drink, which gives their beef a marbling effect. The best part of sukiyaki is that you have to cook everything yourself. Oil goes in the pan, then the veg and the meat, and it all sizzles away over a table burner. Everyone has a bowl containing one raw egg, and the food is taken from the pan, dunked into the egg, then popped into the mouth - all using chopsticks. Delicious!

### John:

*On one of our nights off in Tokyo the band ended up in a Korean restaurant. We eventually tottered out of there, and - wonder of wonders! - there on a balcony opposite was a group of girls smiling and waving at us. Maybe it was the effects of the gallons of saki we'd consumed, but Ken decided to do a Rudolph Valentino and climb up to 'rescue' them. The only way he could do this was by first getting on Vic's back, then up the latticework for the final stretch onto the balcony. But just when he reached the point of no return, so to speak, an angry-looking male face*

*suddenly appeared behind those of the girls. Ken let go his grip sharply*
*and fell back onto Vic. Both collapsed in the roadway, and then we all*
*beat a hasty retreat.*

*Back at the hotel Ken entered Dave's room carrying a large potted*
*palm that he'd found outside in the corridor. Dave solemnly accepted the*
*plant and walked out of his room with it. Ron Weatherburn happened to*
*be passing, so he took the plant off Dave and put it into the lift. All this*
*was conducted straight-faced and in silence; no one uttered a word.*
*Finally, Weathers pressed every button in the lift, including the alarm*
*bell. Whoever was next to use that lift would've found it apparently*
*being operated by a triffid! Childish, maybe, but all good clean fun.*

### Kenny:

We travelled everywhere in Japan on the bullet train. These
trains only stop for two minutes and would set off again whether
you'd got on it or were still on the platform, so sometimes you'd
be left behind. Of course, we had all our cases, the drums, bass
and other things to take with us, so our roadie had to get all that
on the train within two minutes – and, if he was lucky, he'd get
on too! Inside there was a kilometre meter, so you knew how fast
you were going. It went up to about 300kph.

When we went to Hokkaido, which is the northernmost
island, we flew there. Nobody spoke a word of English and there
were no English signs or anything familiar to us whatsoever. All
the restaurant menus were in Japanese, so if we wanted
something to eat we usually ended up with some kind of Jap
spaghetti bolognese. In the outside windows of restaurants they
had plates of what looked like real food, but it was plastic. Even
the fried eggs looked lifelike. On second thoughts, it probably
was real food, only covered in plastic! These were stacked up in
the window displays, so you could go and point to what you
fancied. There were never any potatoes anywhere - so we had
no chips. We all lost weight (I must remember to eat rice at all

135

times!) The whisky was awful, and the toilets were just holes in the ground. The only words of Japanese I knew were "Domo arigato", which means, "Thank you very much".

**John:**

*One evening Shigai, our Japanese road manager, arranged a special treat for us - a party attended by real geisha girls. So there we were, sitting cross-legged in our robes and sandals at a long, low table, when three middle-aged geishas entered, each one carrying a long-necked Japanese banjo. During the recital we were all invited to join in the choruses and, determined not to lose face, we crooned nonsensically in time with the twanging accompaniment. Our bizarre singalong was suddenly interrupted when a phone rang. One of the geisha 'girls' put down her instrument and rose to answer it. "If that's Geraldo," said Ron Bowden, "tell him I've already got a gig tonight!"*

**Kenny:**

Sunday was usually our day off, and in the morning we'd be taken on a tour of a Buddhist shrine. In the evening we'd be taken for meal, and then on to a strip show. By the end of that tour we were all well acquainted with Japanese strip shows, so now I can say for certain that nothing of importance goes sideways in Japan!

In one of these shows, during what might be called the second act, workmen came on stage behind the girls and started to haul out great chunks of scenery, making a tremendous racket. The strippers shouted at them to stop the noise, as though they thought the audience was there just to listen to the music! It ended in a flurry of naked bodies, bits of scaffolding and a huge cardboard mock-up of a water garden tipping slowly forwards into the front rows of the audience. Quite a finale!

**John:**

At the end of the Japanese tour in 1964 we should've gone on to Manila, where we had a gig booked at the US base. However, it was called off at the last minute, as trouble had flared up in Vietnam and the base was empty of troops. We were sent to Okinawa instead to play cabaret in another US army base.

After the show I was waylaid by a granite-faced, leathery old military drunk, who was completely bonkers. He told me he was planning to invade Australia with a task force of 12 men. I didn't catch the reason why, but as he seemed to be waiting for my opinion I said that was okay by me. Maybe something got lost in translation; at any rate, he seemed to be under the impression that I'd volunteered to be in his team.

"How's your parachuting experience, son?" he demanded, fixing me with a steady ice-blue gaze.

"Well …"

"We're in a 'go' situation right now! Understand?"

"Oh yes," I said. Oh no! I thought.

Fortunately, I was saved in the nick of time from being press-ganged into World War Three by the intervention of a Japanese hostess, who had my interests at heart. "Your friends are leaving NOW," she said, with a knowing wink. "I think you'd better go." I did!

**Kenny:**

We did another tour of Japan in 1972, and I arranged for Mina, my drummer Ron Bowden's wife, and my wife to meet us out there. They arrived a bit the worse for wear, as their flight took a very roundabout route and kept stopping all over the place. Eventually, they got to Tokyo and we booked them in the Tokyo Prince Hotel. We were all on the fifth floor. Ron Bowden was about three doors down the corridor from Betty and me, in a room next to the lift. While I was dozing on the bed, Betty went outside to check the lock on the door. The trouble was she was only wearing her knickers and bra. While she was outside she let

137

go of the door and it shut behind her, locking her out. Well, I was fast asleep by then and she couldn't wake me by knocking on the door, so she decided to go along to Ron and Mina's room. As she was trying to attract Mina's attention by rapping on their door, the lift arrived and the doors opened. Half a dozen Japanese gentlemen walked out to find this lovely blonde lady, half naked, standing in front of them. So they all started bowing to her, while she was covering up her nether regions as best as she could. It was bloody hilarious. She's a bit scatty to say the least.

### John's Journal: Tokyo, 1972

#### 5 May

*It was a night off tonight, and at 8 p.m. everyone assembled at the hotel, undecided as to what to do. Ron Bowden mentioned that he'd discovered a pub with a dartboard while roaming around this morning. We considered that for a while in silence. Eventually, John Parker said we must all be mad to come to the other side of the world just to go to a pub with a dartboard.*

*Nevertheless, we do like our simple pleasures, so darts it is. We were all set to go when Ted Baldwin, our banjo/guitarist, exclaimed, "What shall I do with my monkey?" He had purchased this furry electronic toy that repeatedly bangs a pair of cymbals together, and will only stop banging if you hit it on the head. "Stuff it up your arse," offered Ron Bowden helpfully. Instead, Ted left his monkey in the care of one of the hotel receptionists, who accepted it inscrutably. Out in the street, as the revolving doors spun behind us, we heard the faint clash of tiny cymbals, then the thud, followed by laughter. "Oh, they'll have fun with that," said Ted Baldwin in a sort of kindly, motherly way - as though he was setting off for a hen party and leaving the kids to amuse themselves.*

*The 'pub' was truly Oriental - a bamboo-and-paper shack, and for several seconds we stood in its low doorway gaping in mute wonder. The dartboard was more like an archery target, set up only a couple of feet above floor level. Fifteen feet away a group of Japs was ferociously hurling darts at it like Samurai warriors. The barman came across to us, arms outstretched. "Sorree, closed," he said. Seeing what was going on inside we took his word for it, but as we left an Oriental hand plucked Ken's sleeve: "You want bar, Johnny?" "Be British, Ken," I whispered to him. "Pretend you haven't heard." But by then pimps were swirling round Ken like worker bees around the queen. They left the rest of us alone. It looked as though they'd already figured out who was carrying all the money!*

*Eventually we found a bar that would let us in. It was an underground place with low lighting. Inside, we mistook the barman for an off-duty sumo wrestler, and he mistook all of us for a British football team. We tried to explain who we were. "Ah, Sukiyaki," breathed the fat barman, in sudden understanding, "Washington Square."*

*"Midnight in Moscow," replied Ken, "Samantha." At least they had found a common language.*

*"You sumo?" said Ken, pointing to the barman's colossal paunch. The barman laughed and didn't stop laughing for a while. It turned out the only wrestling he had ever done was the arm kind, but, as he then indicated he wanted to take us all on, we got the impression he might be good at it. We selected Vic Pitt as our representative, as he has strong bass player's wrists. Vic did win the opening contest but lost the second and third. Clarinettist Andy Cooper was extremely grieved that our lad had been beaten by "a Jap rat", and didn't get over it for the rest of the night.*

*The following day Ian, our roadie, rang his girlfriend in England. She told him that Leeds had beaten Arsenal 1-0 in the Cup Final. This means that at the same time as our families in England were sitting in armchairs on a sunny afternoon watching Leeds score their winning goal the Kenny Ball band would have been downing late evening vodkas in the basement of a sleazy Tokyo bar. It's a funny old world.*

## Kenny:

In 1965 we drove through Frankfurt for the first time in six years. We spent some time searching for the Storyville Club, where the band started to get going back in 1959. We found it at last, and it was like taking a step back in time. Everything inside was still the same, except that a beat group was rehearsing on stage instead of a trad jazz band. But the old posters were still up there on the walls. John Marshall, the owner, was absent, so we had one beer and left for our destination - a club in Mannheim where we'd be playing three sets between 9.30 p.m. and 3 a.m. over the next few days. We went there for a rehearsal and found that Beryl Bryden was on with us. She wouldn't rehearse, she said, because she had an appointment at the hairdressers!

## John:

*Beryl eventually turned up for rehearsal, and I noticed that somehow she'd managed to squeeze herself into a voluminous pair of white trousers. While I was warming up, blowing a few tentative notes on the old trombone, in my mind I was picturing Beryl's washing line under a full load: like the Cutty Sark setting sail for the Orient.*

*When the gig was over, Vic and I raided the deserted kitchen and stole some cold potatoes. While we were there, Beryl loomed out of the semi-darkness and invited me to accompany her to a club where, she said, "the waitress laid her tits on the table".*

*"Last night Dave Jones tried to stab them with his fork," she said.*

*"How romantic," I replied, and then politely declined.*

*I remembered that Lou, the bass player with the German supporting band, had professed a fondness for large women, so I arranged for him to introduce himself to Beryl while I slipped out of the kitchen.*

**Kenny:**

After the gig Bill Bowyer and I went out to eat. Bill, who thinks he can speak very good German, ordered "Ein bier" at the top of his voice. A few moments later a bottle of Coke and a hunk of bread was delivered to him. He said he would never try to speak to the natives again in their own language!

**John:**

*People might consider us staid old gentlemen these days, but I'm ashamed to say we must have presented a rather less comfortable image back on that 1965 tour of Germany. Take these extracts from my journal:*

### John's Journal: Germany, 1965

#### Monday 15 February

*Hamburg. We moved into the City Hotel near the station. An awful, dingy place.*

*It is a night off tonight, so Ken, Bill Bowyer, Paddy Lightfoot and I strolled to the Zillertal; a sort of Bavarian beer cellar. Dave Jones and Vic Pitt were already there when we arrived and we ordered foaming half-litres of beer.*

*We were joined by a crowd of British merchant seamen, led by 'Bosun', a broken-nosed, red-bearded character. Beer was flowing everywhere by the time Ken volunteered to conduct the Bavarian band, just visible through the smoke haze at the far end of the long hall. For the privilege of being allowed to conduct, Ken had to buy beer for all the band (the German band, that is, not ours!) After a while I got the impression that our large and raving British contingent was making the locals a bit apprehensive. It came to a head when we were all ejected from the place for dancing on the tables.*

*Outside we staggered around in the freezing cold. Bill Bowyer solemnly announced he was going to end it all here and now, and* laid himself down across the tramlines. Not realising he was stretched out in front of me I tripped full length over him. Others tripped over me, and soon all of us were spreadeagled in the centre of Hamburg High Street, waving our limbs feebly like upturned woodlice. Some instinctive patriotic urge caused us to squirm around to form into the pattern of the Union Jack. Luckily no trams came along.

Nor were any staff present in our hotel, so Paddy Lightfoot for some reason thought it a good idea to grab a handful of magazines, tear them into shreds and throw them around like confetti. Upstairs we charged down corridors, kicking the pairs of shoes that were laid neatly outside doors. Bill Bowyer spewed up in his sink, forgetting to take the plug out first. He seemed quite concerned about this, but someone advised him to forget all about it and sort it out in the morning. "What do you mean, sort it out!?" he said in horror, and was promptly sick again; though this time he had the presence of mind to open his room door to make sure it all went outside on the corridor carpet.

I found it difficult to get into the room I was sharing with Paddy. My ankle bones, it seemed, were connected to my shoulder bones.

### Tuesday 16 February

The hotel manager shook me awake. He looked irate and was shouting. I glanced beyond him at the maid, who was glaring at me. "Schweine!!" she snarled, and the pair of them left, slamming the door. A second or so later the door was violently flung open again and the manager with spit running down his chin roared, "'PIGS!!!" just to make sure we got the message. I told him to pick on someone his own size, and then tried to get back to sleep. No chance. Once again the door opened: "Bloody bastards!!" screamed the manager, and slammed the door, a little harder this time. Paddy was now awake too, looking bleary and ill. Others were shambling about in the corridor in various stages of undress. Bill's face looked

*oddly crumpled - as though it had been immersed in water all night.*
*Ken was blinking. A few minutes later we were all standing in the*
*street outside the hotel in silence, our suitcases lying all around us*
*where they had been flung by the hotel staff. Now we have to find*
*another hotel. "Who won the war anyway?" somebody growled.*

### Kenny:

In 1962 the band went to America for the first time. It was a two-week spot in Bob Scobey's club in Chicago (trumpeter Bob Scobey's band was touring Britain on an exchange programme). Our audiences were very receptive; in fact, they went potty each night, and the manager told us we were the best band he'd ever seen. He probably said that to all the fellas.

### John:

*We also learned that all clubs in Chicago were run by 'The Syndicate'.*
*I can't vouch for the truth of that, but for what it's worth I did notice*
*that one of the club bosses had a mashed-up face and a big cigar. It*
*may be just coincidence, but on the day we arrived the press reported*
*that a body had been found in the boot of a car left abandoned outside*
*the rear door of the club. And earlier somebody had been shot dead in*
*a barber's shop - so in that fortnight I started growing my hair long!*
*One night the barman said to me, grinning, "Have you been shot at*
*yet?" Oh well; maybe it was all just a big joke.*

*We also played at New York's Metropole - the famous jazz club,*
*which was not as high-class as I'd expected from its reputation. The*
*band was set up on a stage about five feet high, situated behind a long*
*bar. It wasn't really a jazz audience: people were perched on high*
*stools at the bar and usually they just popped in for a quick one before*
*moving on. On the plus side, the house band was led by legendary*
*drummer Gene Krupa! He was a real gent; he even waited at the*
*bottom of the stairs while we descended from the dressing room, and*
*then held the door open for us.*

*Kenny:*

Of course, there were loads of groupies around back then. In Chicago in 1962 I teamed up with a waitress. I can't remember her name - but I do remember her body! Isn't that an awful thing to say? Back in England - especially during the Trad Boom - it was the same thing. At the Hundred Club in Oxford Street, London, there used to be a girl called Kate who did it for everyone. We used to call her 'Forni-Kate'. If I remember right, she used to scratch everybody with her long nails - leave her mark as it were - all the way down your back. You used to have to wear a shirt all the time when you went home! But it was another notch on her bedpost. Then, of course, there were the ones that George Melly talked about in his book, *Owning Up*. The one he called 'Mucky Alice' we all knew as 'Bradford Alice'. In fact, our pianist Johnny Parker took a shine to Alice, and I have a feeling he had her living with him for a while.

Then there was Jeannie Jurd, who lived near Bondi Beach in Australia. Jeannie was a great jazz fan and a terrific lady, but she was a groupie sure enough. Dave Jones fell in love with her and shacked up with her for a while. And she was really the jazzman's friend. She had lots of lovers - in particular, American jazzmen. Anyway, about 20 years ago we arrived late at night in Sydney and Jeannie's flat above a music shop on Bondi Beach was not far from where we were staying.

My new wife, Michelle, was travelling with me, and I said to her, "You've got to come and see my friend Jeannie." So we went up the stairs to her flat on the first floor and knocked on the door, and I heard Jeannie say, "Who is it?"

"Kenny Ball," I said.

Well, she opened the door wearing a nightshirt and as she said, "Kenny, how are you?" she lifted her shirt right up over her head. She was stark naked. And me with my new wife by my side! My face dropped, but luckily Michelle is no prude and we fell about.

Anyhow, in we went and had a couple of drinks, and Jeannie said, "Go and help yourself to another in the cupboard."

So I opened the cupboard and saw all these matchboxes. And this is absolutely true - every matchbox had a label with a name written on it! Jeannie, every time she'd screwed somebody, had snipped off some of their pubic hair, put it in a matchbox and marked their name on it! She'd kept them all; dozens of them. There was Duke Ellington, Louis Armstrong and his All Stars, Count Basie's band, Lionel Hampton's ...

Jeannie's still alive and I phoned her a couple of months ago. She must be well into her eighties now. I once wrote a song about her called 'The Oldest Living Roadie in the World'.

She did get married to a man called Napier, but now she's gone back to her own name, Jeannie Jurd. She'd had a hell of an upbringing and opened her heart to us once; a really kind lady with a heart of gold, who just loved her jazz and her jazz musicians as well - and kept mementos of all of them!

I invited Jeannie to come and stay with us at Stansted and she almost took over the house. She stayed six weeks. She often made us a big salad, and I noticed she chopped up the lettuce. Chopping up lettuce was virtually unheard of in those days, and I got to like it done that way. One day my old dad came round for lunch and he noticed I was chopping up lettuce for the salad.

He said, "'I've never seen anyone do that before, son."

I replied, "Oh, it's one of the things the Australians do."

"Blimey, Ken, you're turning into the Galloping Gourmet," he responded. Lovely old boy, my dad.

Then there was this striptease dancer in New Zealand. At that time they were very strict with the drinking laws over there and really everything was very respectable and ultra right-wing. So the only place we found where we could get a drink was in a nightclub. A couple of the band and I went along and I met this striptease dancer there. I started chatting with her and she seemed very friendly, and we joined in some 'connubial' fun. Then she said, "Where're you going next?" Well, from that night on she came with us all the way round New Zealand, which made me very happy.

When we got back to Auckland we should've been flying straight on to Honolulu, but our pianist Ron Weatherburn couldn't get a visa because he suffered from epilepsy and they wouldn't let him into America. So my roadie Bill Bowyer had to stay behind with Ron in Auckland while we set off for America, where we were due to play some dates. Bill would have to spend a lot of time rushing around the Embassies trying to get Ron a special visa and re-route him through Canada or wherever. Obviously we couldn't afford the best hotels for them, so I put Bill and Ron in a smaller one, where they shared a twin room.

Anyhow, my New Zealand girlfriend, the striptease artist, was up for anything, so I said, "We've got to go, but would you mind looking after my mate Bill? He's just got over a divorce and he's very low, and Ron Weatherburn, well, he's all right by himself." So there were Bill and Ron in this twin-bedded room and the only heating they had was a single-bar electric fire. Ron Weatherburn said to me later, "You left us, and we were there two nights and I've never heard anything like it. There was I in my bed trying to sleep, and by the light of the electric fire all I could see was dancing images on the ceiling, the floors and the walls and this grunting and groaning, shrieking and moaning all night. I never want to share a room with that bloke ever again in my life."

The end of the story is that my poor little striptease girl married an Australian sheep farmer, who had thousands of acres of land in Australia. Then he died and left her all the money. A few years later we went back to Sydney and she turned up to see us in a huge car with a wonderful fur coat - everything. That's life!

### John's Journal: New Orleans, 1963

**28 September**

*We changed planes at Georgia, where we saw Fats Domino in a bright yellow silk suit strolling by. At New Orleans an old lady ran out in front of us and unrolled a red carpet for us to walk on. We had quarter of an hour to get shaved and then on to a TV show. Our gig started at midnight, after which we had a tour of the old bars. I stood on a corner and heard Dixieland jazz coming from all around. We called in at a club where Santo Pecora's band was playing (I remember buying a record of that band when I was still at school - a Parlophone blue label 78rpm). Tonight Santo loaned me his trombone and I sat in with his band! He told me that Jack Teagarden had been working across the street once and he'd stuck his trombone out of the door and kept blowing until the people came. It's an old jazz myth that seems to apply to every legendary musician of the past. Ron Weatherburn put our thoughts into words in his airmail letter that was published in Melody Maker: "It's hot, tropically hot, and I'm sitting on the patio of the old Absinthe House - on the corner of Bourbon and Bienville - in the process of recovering after the three most hectic and most wonderful days of my life ... Kenny is 'King' of New Orleans at the moment, nothing less. He has only to walk into a bar or club to be recognised, announced and given an ovation. He can do no wrong, and neither can the entire band for that matter ... One night, in the King's Room on Herville Street, Armand Hug played a solid hour of Jelly Roll Morton in my honour. How about that!"*

### Kenny:

One of our US tours took in San Francisco. The highlight for us was Earthquake McGoons, a jazz club run by Turk Murphy, a trombone player. He was a wonderful chap, who was one of the original Yerba Buena band, and he had this dreadful stammer, but he was a smashing bloke. We played there for a couple of nights. And one of the greatest compliments he ever paid me was when he said, "Would you be my trumpet player? I can pay you $300 a week." That was in the early 1960s. Of course, at that point I'd just got the band on a world tour, I'd got hit records for us, and it would've meant ditching everybody, so I said, "No thanks. It's very nice of you." But I've always remembered it, because he was one of the great jazz trombone players, very much a Kid Ory man, and he wanted me to be his trumpet player. I suppose $300 a week was a lot of money then, come to think about it. I might've taken the job now, but I don't think so. Glad I didn't, because it led to some other things.

### John's Journal: USA, 1965

**Sunday 9 May**
*Today we flew by charter flight from Jackson, Mississippi, to Columbia, South Carolina. The band and its luggage were distributed among three small Piper aircraft, the pilots of which entertained us before take-off with hair-raising tales of their past stunts, punctuated by graphic descriptions of the various catastrophes that have befallen innocents like ourselves, who have put their trust in daredevil flying cowboys like them.*
*One of these pilots, I thought, looked far too young to be flying anything more substantial than a rubber-powered balsa wood model plane, and what's more, his anecdotes about aeronautical disasters all seemed to be personal ones. I was not impressed with the tales of daredevil zooming over fog-capped peaks either; after all, it was not so long ago that country singer Jim Reeves zoomed into a mountain instead of over it! But it is too late now; it looks like Alan Freeman*

*will be granted his wish to issue our black-bordered LP!*

*I am sitting in the tiny cockpit wedged in by suitcases. The first plane taxis along the runway and makes a sudden U-turn back to the fuel area - it transpired that this pilot had forgotten to top up his crate!*

*Once airborne, the planes got together in a tight V-formation like a squadron of World War Two Mustangs. Our plane was a four-seater, shared by Ken, Dave Jones, myself, and a stack of luggage and instruments in the back. Gene, our pilot, was the young one - too young for this job and a touch too overenthusiastic for my liking. Judging by the whoops and rebel yells we could hear over the intercom, the other two pilots were obviously having a great time too. "Get that thundercloud way over there?" - this was the leader speaking – "Looks deadly, huh?"*

*I glanced apprehensively at Gene, who had a devilish grin on his face. "Whoooo-haaaaa!" he yelled. Our formation then banked sharply and headed straight for a mass of black vapour that looked as solid as Table Mountain. Moments later we were in darkness, bobbing around like corks. There followed some rather more serious lurching, during which my trombone case parted company from the rest of the baggage and socked me one in the back of the neck.*

*Light-headed and seeing stars, I was beginning to wonder what my chances were of applying for a job in the brass section of Glenn Miller's Celestial Big Band, when suddenly we were soaring out into sunlight and clear blue sky, still in perfect V-formation, skimming over tree-covered slopes and whoo-haaaing along with our hosts. Gene was chuckling. "Jeez," he confided, "I don't mind telling you that made me damn scared!" Could have fooled me.*

*Our leader really had been a fighter pilot during the war, and by all accounts he was a hero. He certainly looked heroic now, banking out into sunlight ahead of us. Suddenly it did seem to be fun after all - until Ken was invited to take over the joystick of our aircraft. Why call it a joystick? Wielded by Ken it became the stick from hell!*

*That night's show and the accompanying live recording had been* arranged by George H Buck Jr, long-time jazz enthusiast and owner of Jazzology Records. "I can honestly state," he writes in the sleeve notes, "that to date, in my jazz lifetime, this concert presented on Mother's Day in 1965 by Kenny Ball was truly the most exciting and thrilling jazz concert I have ever attended."

Harry Godwin, another great jazz enthusiast, added, "Kenny didn't forget it was Mother's Day … he offered 'My Mother's Eyes', pleasing those lucky Carolinians as he explained to them in his Ronald Coleman-like British accent that "we love this day in England, too."

### Kenny:

At the end of the American part of the tour we flew from Los Angeles to Sydney, Australia. We changed planes at Sydney and eventually arrived at Perth about two hours before our concert was due to start. I had to rush around doing radio shows to advertise the concert, and then it was straight on stage. The band on before us was a rock 'n' roll group. They were good musicians but, of course, were playing a very different style to us. The audience had come to see us and didn't give them a good reception. I felt so sorry for them.

Anyhow, we went down a storm even though we were absolutely knackered. Our next trip was early next morning, to Adelaide. We were playing in a different city each night for two weeks. In other words the promoter made a flipping fortune, as everything was sold out. And he wanted to save money by not having to stay anywhere that would cost him a hotel. I'd never do that again. Never, never. I'd sooner go without than do another tour like that. It was like overnight to Adelaide, and then going around doing radio shows, then immediately on to Sydney, then to Tasmania. We were on the go day after day after day. When I tried to blow trumpet in Sydney - I'll never forget it - I couldn't get a note out. Eventually, I managed to squeak

150

through a couple of notes. It was the beginning of probably a year or so of absolute crap for me, playing-wise. But the band carried me through. I've got to give them credit - they did everything. I couldn't even blow a middle C. Those that are musically inclined will know that's a pretty low note, but I just couldn't hit it. The only way I could get it was to drink half a bottle of bloody gin before I started! And that has frightened me for years. At last I got over it, whatever it was, basically by breath control. This was a yoga breathing exercise, which is holding the breath for a count of eight, and then walking eight paces, gradually letting a bit of the air out each time. And that worked; believe me it did. At least I got over it. I tried to get over the drinking, too, but I'm not quite so sure about that. At least I've definitely cut down a hell of a lot.

### John's Journal: Aussie tour, 1974

*Went out boozing last night. Started off at Tramps accompanied by a wild Scotsman called Les and promoter Dick Lean's son, Dave. Three girls came in and Les whispered into my ear, "They're gobblers." I peered at the girls with renewed interest. I found out later that Dave was referring to the fact that they were dancers at a nightclub called Gobblers.*

*The conversation at the bar is colourful. "Course 'e does," someone is saying. "Stands out like a dog's bollocks, don't it?"*

*"Haven't set eyes on him," says another, "since he was knee high to an Abbo's Y-fronts."*

*After a few more jars I attempted my own version of this Aussie-ese. "Lorst me roo!" I exclaimed loudly to no one in particular. "Me billabong's gone crook and me wallaby's rat-shit."*

*Fortunately, no one was listening. For me, travel hysteria has set in earlier than usual. It would help if I could take time off to sleep. Trouble is it's too easy to fall into the Aussie habit of talking nineteen to the dozen about nothing at all. Once you start you can't stop. Last night, I did just that; instead of going to bed at a reasonable hour I knocked back a large jar of Aussie plonk while chatting to an English science teacher and his Aussie girlfriend. I got to bed at 4.30 a.m. and was up for brekkers at 6.30 a.m.*

*We arrived in Launceston, Tasmania, where a grumpy hotel receptionist and damp beds rounded off the day nicely. I struggled through a dry piece of fried chicken that tore off the bone in long spaghetti-like strands. The concert was in an old town hall where the audience sat upright on wooden seats, clad in woollies and overcoats, shivering. Ken nodded amicably to the leader of the other band, a fat trombonist with close-set eyes. In reply to Ken's polite query as to whether he lived here in Launceston, the trombonist said warily, "Are you trying to fraternise with us?"*

*After the concert I went back to my room and watched TV. There was an old Joe Brown film on. It was called 'What a Crazy World'.*

### 11 September, Albany, Australia

*Got to bed at 1a.m. Up 5.30 a.m., bleary-eyed and optimistic. An angry snarl from the twin engines of the Fokker Friendship as it prepared to assault the skies, laden with half-awake businessmen and hungover musicians.*

*"Good morning," I said brightly to the air hostess.*

*"What's good about it?" was her deadpan reply.*

*I drank my way steadily through the concert and saw that the rest of the band are looking just as jaded as I feel. Everyone's eyes look as if they're halfway down their faces. My attendance at the inevitable function afterwards was the shortest ever; I entered through the front door of the pub, took note of all the ear-bashers waiting to pounce, and just kept on walking, into the gents and out the back door. Feeling hungry, I called in at the 'Sea Fry' and went to bed with fish and chips. Ah, the romantic life of a roaming troubadour!*

## 12 September, Melbourne

*We'd just come off stage when Rolf Harris put his head round the dressing room door. "Who wants to learn the breathing trick?" he asked. He was carrying a didgeridoo and there was blue paint all round the edges of his fingernails and crevices in the skin of his hands.*

*Rolf Harris uses an old Aborigine trick when he blows a long continuous note on the didgeridoo, apparently without taking a breath. He showed us how it was done. "It looks like it's against the laws of nature," he said. To practise it you took a mouthful of water and expelled it in a steady stream while breathing in through the nose. It's similar to, but far more difficult, than, patting your head while making circular motions on your tummy. He demonstrated on the didgeridoo. It was an eerie sound - if you were to hear a dozen of those droning away out in the bush at night you'd run for your life.*

*I tried this circular breathing act, but once again I couldn't get it at all. Rolf obviously didn't remember, but I had tried the trick before on Rolf's didgeridoo a few years back on 'Saturday Night at the Mill'. I reminded him of this, and that he'd played his, then, latest single 'Yarrabanjee'. "Jesus," he said, "I'd completely forgotten that song too."*

## John's Journal: Australia, 1986

### 9 April

*The senior musicians hung one on last night. That is our elderly drummer Ron Bowden, Alan Geddes, another old drummer, and 72-year-old Aussie bandleader Graeme Bell. Graeme had spotted a bottle behind the bar whose label read 'Fuck'. It doesn't matter how old a jazz musician is, he's still a young kid at heart. "I'd like a fuck please," Graeme said politely to the barmaid. She'd obviously heard it all before and poured him one. It must have been powerful stuff.*

*Soon Graeme was returning again to the bar. "Give us a fuck," he*
*yelled. Later still he was rolling up to the bar yelling at the top of his*
*voice: "HOW ABOUT ANOTHER FUCK THEN!!"*

*It was the sort of childish joke, said Alan Geddes, that you have to*
*pay for. In more ways than one. Graeme was not quite himself this*
*morning. "He usually ties one on about once a week," Bob Barnard,*
*his trumpet player, whispered to me. "But it has its compensations -*
*he's quieter the next morning."*

*[Graeme is an amazing fellow. At the last count (2011) he had*
*turned 97 and was still as perky as ever. I wonder if he still has a*
*'Fuck'?]*

### Kenny:

Hong Kong was a beautiful place. We had a lovely time there
and played in a couple of hotels. And once we played in the
Hong Kong Jazz Club, which was run by a Chinese trumpet
player that loved having jazz bands passing through. We didn't
get a lot of money for it, but we had a night off, so we said we'd
play. We had to change in the bloody kitchen. There were
waiters coming in and out calling for 'One Hung Lo' or
something, while we were taking our trousers off. Anyway, when
we went on to play it was lovely. The people were so
enthusiastic; it was terrific.

### John:

*In Hong Kong our roadie, Pete Barnard, bought some Snake Penis Oil*
*and some Snake Wine to rejuvenate the parts other snake oils can't*
*reach. According to John Benson that was "a load of old cobras."*

### Kenny:

In New Zealand on our 1967 tour I always used to get a chuckle
out of reading the newspaper reviews of our concerts. The
reviewers must have spent all their time in the bar instead of

watching the concert. I remember one paper claiming we'd played Faithful Hussar very well; a number we have never played in our lives. Another journalist went into ecstasies over the piano playing of Ron Weatherburn, who was not with us on that tour. Ron was back home in England nursing the stitches in his hand after falling off his bike.

### John's Journal: New Zealand, 1967

#### Friday 6 October

*I strolled down Hamilton High Street in the morning and met John Parker (our dep pianist on this tour in place of Ron Weatherburn) coming up from the opposite direction. We stood a while chatting, during which John Parker confessed to me that he had fallen instantly and passionately in love with a Maori girl who had smiled at him on this street. "Trouble is," he added, "I don't have the courage just to walk up to her and ask her out for a date. What should I do?"*

*"Easy," I told him. "Just waylay her and keep talking without letting her get a word in edgeways - you're good at that."*

*"But what if she doesn't speak English?" enquired John.*

*I said that would be the least of his worries, and then went on to tell him about the Italian girl with jet-black hair and blue eyes I once picked up in London the day after I was demobbed from National Service. She hardly spoke English, but I did find out that her father owned a cafe in East Finchley.*

*"Just charge in and turn on the charm," I bragged. "You'll find it'll work wonders. The very next morning I had cycled over to her father's café ..." I broke off, staring blankly into space: memory had returned.*

*"Yes?" prompted John, "then what happened?"*

*"All her family came out and stared at me until I went away."*

*"Oh," said John.*

*Seeing as I wasn't on the right track there, I told him about another time I had picked up a girl in the street. I was with the Terry Lightfoot band at the time and we had just done a gig in Skegness. Paddy Lightfoot and I had downed quite a few pints and were walking back down the road from the pub when we bumped into two girls. That night it was my turn for the ugly one, but being fairly plastered this didn't matter to me at all. Not until the effects started to wear off, that is. That's when I realised I was in a clinch with Dracula's daughter on a park bench in the rain, and the bandwagon had left without us. By that time we were all soaked to the skin, so we tried knocking on a few hotel doors. None of the worthy hotel proprietors of Skegness would have anything to do with such a disreputable-looking quartet, so to get out of the rain we found a bus shelter and sat huddled together on the wet pavement, shivering. I vaguely recall that sometime during the night a policeman came by and shone his torch on us …*

*"What's up?" I said, seeing that John Parker was frowning at me.*

*"You know what?" he said, after a moment's thought. "You've convinced me: I'm going to have a wank instead."*

### Kenny:

Forty years ago there wasn't much to do during the day in these Antipodean realms other than go to the pictures. Fortunately, our promoters were Kerridge Odeon, who owned most of the cinemas in NZ, so we got free tickets in every town. Most of the band were in the cinema to see Thoroughly Modern Millie, which turned out to be quite a giggle. The place was empty apart from us, and we sat in the circle having a whale of a time - as the photo in the local newspaper showed.

### John's Journal: New Zealand, 1967

#### 13 October, Wellington

*Off to Wellington. Wellington is the windy city. It is no place for* descending aeroplanes, it tries to chuck them back. Landing in an Ansett DC3 at Wellington airport is like being thrown about on a blanket. Our poor old ex-wartime Dakota should have earned a dignified retirement many years ago instead of being forced to hover stock still, quivering, in midair like a sparrowhawk. When it was not standing still it was dropping like a stone. We hit bottom several times - not at ground level, fortunately, but onto a trampoline of compressed air that felt every bit as solid. Then we would rise up rapidly; the tiny, fragile wings flapping like a seabird taking off from an oil slick with a beak-full of overweight plankton. There was a constant squealing, whining and drumming coming from outside, as though a giant was running his fingernails down the fuselage. Terry 'I-Will-Never-Fly-Again' Lightfoot downed half a bottle of gin while we lurched between three and five thousand feet, and we amused ourselves by hanging on to the seats in front and making daft remarks about forthcoming posthumous hit albums with black borders. At an angle of 45 degrees the pilot tried for the umpteenth time to come in on a wing and a prayer and at last managed to get one wheel down. We held our breath for half a minute until the other wheel crunched down sickeningly, then joined in a heartfelt round of applause for the pilot.

### 14 October, Auckland

Flying by Pan Am 707 was a vastly different experience than the Ansett flights we had got used to over the past couple of weeks. Everything was very smooth and cool, particularly the US air hostesses. They were staying on in Auckland and invited us to a party in the hotel after the gig.

It's amazing how one's first opinions of people can be turned upside down when you meet them in a different setting. The ice-cool demeanour of the air hostesses was an illusion. At their party in room 818 the only thing ice cool was the ice. The first sight that greeted me as I entered was the flight-deck steward dressed in a blonde wig, *ladies' nightgown and nothing else. The coolest, prettiest air hostess on that flight was dancing, or rather reeling about, on her own. Four Aussie QANTAS stewards were simultaneously and unsuccessfully trying to grope her as she repeatedly staggered past.*

*I glanced around. I saw Ron Bowden waving his arms and looking bleary-eyed, and Ted Baldwin, who was sporting a wide-brimmed Aussie hat. Ian Pickstock, our roadie, was there too, talking seriously to a bored air hostess about quantum theory - or was it QANTAS theory?*

*I strolled over to Ken, the other survivor.*

*"Looks like the Aussies have just been rowed out," said Ken, referring to the state of play. The four Australian groping-stewards were now huddled in a disconsolate group at the far end of the room. Then one of them made one last desperate grab at the prettiest air hostess as she circled past, dancing her solitary dance, and this time managed to whisk her into an adjoining room. The quickness of the hand deceives the eye, I thought. But then the steward re-emerged even quicker, clutching his nether regions, obviously in some pain. Memo: steer clear of pretty American air hostesses.*

*The telephone rang; someone was complaining about the noise. Ken, who had been hoping for a mass orgy, yawned and said he was off to bed. There came a knock at the door: it was the night porter. "I'm afraid," he said, "that you're still making too much noise in here." The prettiest air hostess smiled sweetly at him. "Go fuck yourself," she said, "and while you're at it, bring some more fucking ice."*

*And that was the end of another perfect night.*

### Kenny:

At the Airport terminal everyone was hysterical due to too much alcohol and not enough sleep. Paddy was leaping around like a frog (he said he was a kangaroo). Terry Lightfoot was looking dazed and kept saying, "What went wrong? What am I doing here?" Johnny Parker was stretched out on a wooden bench complaining of palpitations. Everyone seemed a bit doolally, and our fellow travellers back to Blighty weren't impressed, sitting there with stony faces and ignoring us.

### *John:*

*In the 1960s, after one of these Round the World Tours, we'd return home to resume our one-night-stand routine around the British Isles in a sequence of brand-new to start with, but soon clapped-out, motor vehicles. We were in perpetual motion, it seemed; in a constant hurry to leave one place so as to get to the next on time. Our tour bookings always followed the scenic route - for example, Brighton to Eastbourne via Glasgow. It was the opinion of some band cynics that our agents chose the venues by throwing darts at a map of the UK; others felt sure we were the unwitting targets of a newspaper 'Spot The Ball Band' competition!*

*Among all that blur of activity only a few landmarks stand out in my memory, one being the gig of 22 November 1963. On that night the band was playing a concert at the Albert Hall (the Albert Hall, Stirling in Scotland, that is, not London). The concert got off to a fine start, though there was a brief commotion during the first set when an elderly woman blundered in off the street and wandered up the centre aisle to mount the stage. Before the band realised what was happening she'd grabbed the microphone and was yelling into the sound system something about a president having been shot. The lady was quickly ushered away into the wings - these things happen. The disturbance continued offstage, but the woman had left the hall by the interval. We discovered then that her news had been confirmed.*

*It has been said that everyone who was around on the day President Kennedy was assassinated will remember where they were and what they were doing. Around 300 Scottish jazz fans may recall they were sitting in the stalls at the Albert Hall, Stirling, listening to the Kenny Ball Band play a rather chaotic version of 'Muskrat Ramble'.*

# 10
# HERE AND THERE

*John's Journal: Somewhere in Scotland, 1967*

*After the gig Paddy Lightfoot and I, both of us temporarily off the booze, left the others at the bar and took the healthy twenty-minute stroll back to the hotel. When we got there we discovered that neither of us had a front-door key. Never mind, I said, I'll climb in through that half-open window. Paddy gave me a leg-up and I was in. Once inside I found I was in a long boxroom, the door of which was locked on the outside, and there was no light switch. After prowling around in the darkness for a bit I found another window to clamber out through. I was now disoriented as well as half-blind. The hotel was built on a steep slope, and the ground level on one side was almost a storey higher than on the other. Hanging by my fingertips from the windowsill like Harold Lloyd, it occurred to me that I didn't know which side of the hotel I was on.*

*"How far away is the ground?" I yelled to Paddy.*

*"Not far," he yelled back. His voice sounded suspiciously distant. My fingertips were getting numb.*

*"You mean just - like - let go?" I ventured.*

*"Yes," Paddy replied, "just let go."*

*"You sure?"*

*"Course I'm sure. Let go."*

*Knowing Paddy's taste for practical jokes, I hung on until I couldn't feel my fingers at all, then swallowed hard and let go. Nothing happened; the ground was only half an inch away.*

*"You might have told me," I grumbled.*

*"I did," said Paddy.*

**Kenny:**

We once played at an Irish club at the far end of Sauchiehall Street in Glasgow. Never again. The promoter even went on stage to assure the audience that we only had one more spot to play - after which he promised that the Irish showband would be back.

### John's Journal: Somewhere in Ireland

*At the soundcheck for the concert last night Ken asked Tony Pitt to play a few choruses of his guitar solo for John Benson's benefit, who hasn't heard it yet. Tony refused. "No point in all that rehearsing bollocks unless we mean to get stuck in right to the end," he said. "When I strum I like to get weaving." Tony has a way with words. It was snowing this afternoon. Tony and I happened to be looking out the hotel window when a horse and cart slowly went by. On the back of the cart was a piano, completely covered in snow. "Bet that's our piano for tonight," said Tony gloomily. "Bound to be," I replied.*

**Kenny:**

That reminds me of that time when Victor Sylvester's band was touring Ireland back in the fifties. Same thing happened: Victor Sylvester was standing by a window looking out when a cart went by carrying two upright pianos. Well, old Victor Sylvester used to use two grand pianos for his strict tempo dance music, and he had an idea that this pair of past-their-prime pianos was meant for his band. So he stormed out and asked the man with the horse if the pianos were for the Victor Sylvester dance that night. The man said yes, so Victor Sylvester told him that these upright pianos were no good - he'd specifically asked for two grand pianos. "Ah, to be sure," said the man, "these are two of the grandest pianos in all Ireland"!

### John's Journal: Somewhere in England

*Ron Bowden, Paddy, Bill Bowyer and myself are sharing one tiny bedroom; I haven't spent a night in digs like this since the days when we used to stay at Mrs Mac's.*

*Mrs Mac's boarding house in the southern suburbs of Manchester was something else. Memories of damp sheets, the pong of cats, the table lampshade so thick with dust that everyone thought it was covered in expensive brown fur. And the picture of the Queen and Prince Philip over the fireplace on which some joker had scrawled, 'Lovely digs; Liz & Phil'.*

*Mrs Mac, with her thick horn-rimmed glasses, resembled bandleader Billy Cotton in drag, and her establishment is long gone; bulldozed off the face of Manchester along with a sizeable portion of the surrounding slum land. No one remembers what became of the lady herself; for all we know she may still be frying eggs under the rubble.*

### John's Journal: Somewhere in Wales, 1973

*Everyone in the band feels bored. Last night we arrived at the stage door of the Double Diamond Club in Caerphilly, knocked, and waited for over five minutes. Eventually Vic Pitt said plaintively, "Do you think they'll let us in if we sing carols?"*

*Later, some of us were sitting at a table, still bored, when a girl approached us. "It's my birthday today," she said chirpily. No one showed any great interest. "'How old do you think I am?" she went on.*

*"Eighteen?" I said, trying to be polite.*

*"No, try again."*

*"Forty-six?" Her face fell.*

*"He meant your bust measurement," said John Parker reassuringly. The girl - who was celebrating her nineteenth birthday - left in a huff. Silence fell again at our table.*

*"I'm still bored," said Andy.*

*"I'm more bored than you are," said John Parker.*

*"I'd go to bed if it wasn't so boring," I said.*

*Vic said, "We could always go outside in the street and mug an old lady."*

### John's Journal: Somewhere in Germany, November 1977

*Princess Anne has just given birth to a baby boy. Ken told tonight's audience, "My Queen is a grandmother." Or so he thought. It transpired that his special form of German translates as 'the queen is a big fat mama'! No wonder the audience had cheered so loudly.*

### John's Journal: Germany

### 27 January 1988

*Ken is pleased with his latest efforts to speak German. Tonight he addressed the audience in a weird dialect that he insisted was 'Hamburg Plat Deutsch' - if that's the correct spelling. The audience seemed to know what he was talking about - which is more than can be said of the band.*

### 28 January

*Ken's 'Hamburg Plat Deutsch' is coming on like a house on fire. His announcement for Duke Ellington's Saturday Night Function emerged as "Samstag abend drinken-poo". The German audience responded in Plat Deutsch too; instead of going Hooray! they went Aaarrgh!!*

*Later Ken asked Karl Lyrman what he thought of his attempts to master the language.*

*"Your German is nowhere country," replied Karl solemnly, "but the people like to hear it all the same."*

*It's the way he tells 'em. "Are the tarts comin' on with the Blumen, then?" enquired Ken backstage, eager to show off some more of his Plat Deutsch.*

*The answer from the stage manager was yes, of course: at the end of the concert girls will indeed walk on stage to present bouquets of flowers to the band.*

### John's Journal: Germany, 1978

*John Benson was telling us about his strange experience last night. After the gig he and Keith Ball, Ken's son, had gone out for an evening stroll. Benson happened to overhear someone mention that Ivy Benson, his namesake, and leader of an all-girl big band, was in town. He decided to investigate, and in a nearby bar he discovered half a dozen of Ivy's girl musicians sitting around a table. Thinking he was onto a good thing, he introduced himself, ordered a drink for himself and Keith and for a while sat among feminine company. He first sensed something was not quite right when the waitress appeared to be in league with the girl musicians. First of all she urged him to buy everyone a drink, including herself, the waitress. He didn't fall for that and was rather surprised when he was presented with a bill for 20 marks. He was even more surprised when the Ivy Benson girls ganged up on him and took the waitress's side.*

*"That's because they're all dykes," broke in Andy. "You walked into a dykes' bar."*

*"Then I hope their fucking vibrator batteries run down," roared Benson.*

*That wasn't the end of his story. The waitress had sent for the police and Benson, who had 16-year-old Keith alongside him, had to beat a swift retreat minus 20 marks. Like he said, it wouldn't have looked too good if he'd been apprehended in a lesbian bar with an underage youth!*

## 12 September

*Karl Lyrman, with his shifty manner, pebble-lensed spectacles and dirty raincoat, looks like an ex-clergyman who's been defrocked for flashing. Karl is, in fact, a German agent - not the spy kind, but the sort who books jazz bands for a living. He is also a bit of a wag. In the TV comedy series Fawlty Towers Basil Fawlty stresses that in the company of Germans one should not mention the War. But in Karl's company you have no choice: World War Two is his only topic of conversation. The War is unfinished business, he claims, because back in 1945 the wrong side had won. It is his opinion that within our lifetime history will repeat itself, only this time with very different results. "You should beware," he would warn us gloomily. "We will not be so lenient next time"!*

*All of which can, of course, be taken with a pinch of salt. During the War, while Karl was serving his Fatherland in the Hitler Youth, he was also a secret fan of the BBC. He and his young cronies spent much of their spare time hiding in a cellar where they listened to dance band broadcasts on their forbidden radio from the Light Programme in London.*

*But it is his 'military experience' with the Hitler Youth that Karl prefers to reminisce about. He usually starts the ball rolling by bringing out of his wallet a dog-eared photo of himself taken in 1943. It shows a skinny fourteen-year-old in an outsize uniform, the top half of his face overshadowed by an enormous steel helmet. In the background is a searchlight and an anti-aircraft gun. Notches have been cut into the barrel of that gun, Karl informs us proudly, each notch representing a hit on a British aircraft. "I hope none of your uncles were in the RAF," he would leer, "as I'm responsible for some British bombers falling from the sky"! Karl also freely admits responsibility for a decisive own goal - the destruction of his home city of Mannheim!*

Karl's war duty was to fire up the generator which powered the searchlights, which in turn enabled the AA gunners to spot their targets. On that one fatal occasion Karl had overslept and missed the signal to start the generator. Consequently the searchlights didn't come on, our RAF uncles in their Lancasters flew on unhindered, and Mannheim was flattened to the ground in a single night. Ever since then Karl has never revisited Mannheim, nor has he ever booked a jazz band into that city.

One morning in a hotel in the city of Cologne I sat at Karl's breakfast table. We were both early risers, and there were just the two of us in the restaurant. Karl began the conversation in his usual way: "If Germany had won the war ..." He broke off, staring into space.

"Yes?" I prompted. Karl, waking from his reverie, pointed at the night porter who was standing rigidly at attention by the door. "If Germany had won the war that man would now be wearing a black uniform and you would not have dared insult him as you did last night."

"I never did!" I replied. "In fact I've never seen him before."

"No?" said Karl. "Well, someone insulted him. It may have been me. He is an arrogant man."

I shot a glance at the night porter, who did appear to be sneering at us.

"You could be right," I said. "He looks like he deserves insulting."

"Or torturing," replied Karl blandly. "For his kind of work fingernails would not be necessary."

Breakfast over, I stood up to leave. "See you soon," I said.

Karl munched his toast and regarded me bleakly. "May be sooner than you think. We still have camps you know ..."!

Who says Germans don't have a sense of humour?


**12 November**

Düsseldorf. Ken announced we were going to play a tune written by

*Irving Berlin.*

*"Remember Berlin?" said Andy, leering evilly at the audience. Then he did a realistic sound impersonation of bombs dropping. The rest of us smiled embarrassedly down at our feet, but the audience remained unconcerned.*

*Later Ken announced the number: 'Putting on the Ritz'. "Ya! Ya!" yelled Andy. "In Berlin we call it PUTTING ON THE BLITZ!!" We are all now sitting in our hotel rooms awaiting a visit from the Gestapo!*

### John's Journal, Germany 1977

*Last night I was speaking to some nice Germans who bought me a beer and made me welcome at their table. One of them spoke very good English. To my shame I still can't speak German, but my interpreter smiled and waved away my embarrassment, saying that in his opinion the reason most Britishers seem shy of practising their German is because Germans do have a vulgar tendency to roar with laughter when they hear their language mispronounced.*

*"I don't blame them," I said.*

*"But you must admit, this is regrettable," persisted my friend apologetically. We considered this for a while.*

*"Oh well," I said, "never mind. C'est la guerre." Oops! Mustn't mention the war! Especially in French!*

### Kenny:

I didn't tell you about 'Mr Sausage' in the West Country, did I? I was one of his favourite musicians and a good friend of his booked me to play for him as a surprise for his birthday party. And Ronnie Scott - who was absolutely at the opposite end of the jazz spectrum to me - was another favourite, so they booked Ronnie as well! So that was that. We had a couple of drinks and went down by train, first class to Bristol. We were picked up by chauffeured limousine and driven to this big tent. It turned out they'd also booked a trad band that didn't have a piano - just two banjos and a drummer. The drummer had this incredible drum kit with a whole row of skulls of different sizes - from a ten-inch one down to about four inches - all mounted on an enormous bass drum. It was so big he had to sit upright and play with his arms up in the air in order to reach the snare drum, which was about six feet from the ground!

Anyhow, when Ronnie and I saw all this, we looked at each other and Ronnie raised his eyebrows.

I said, "What do you want to play?"

He replied, "Fuck all."

So I said, "How does it go?"

Anyway, picture the scene. There we are in this marquee and there's an alcove about four-feet-six across and Ronnie and I are standing by ready to play 'When the Saints Come Marching In'. All of a sudden, there's this yell: "He's here, he's here." Then in comes 'Mr Sausage' in his Rolls Royce. The two banjos get going; the drummer bangs his skulls; there's all this racket going on, and there's Ronnie mumbling, "Oh fuck it, fuck it," under his breath. But the first thing we see on the bonnet of the Rolls Royce isn't the famous 'Flying Lady'. Instead, he had a flying sausage! When Ronnie and I saw it we couldn't play; we just stopped altogether. The bonnet was an extra long one and the chauffeur made several 'laps of honour', so the sausage just kept on coming round until 'Mr Sausage' decided to get out and join the party.

Funnily enough, I saw him at Acker's eightieth birthday party down in Bristol just the other day, and he gave me a couple of pictures of us playing.

**John's Journal:**

### 22 November 1981

*We were at Pebble Mill studios in Birmingham last night for the TV show 'Saturday Night at the Mill', and this morning we were to travel to Bedford. Banjoist John Fenner, having gone into the centre of Birmingham, was late returning and we had to leave without him. Later he told us he had panicked when he realised he would not be back in time, so he hired a cab and asked the driver to take him to the station. "Are you some kind of comedian?" the driver had said. Apparently the station was right in front of him. "How would I know?" said Fenner irritably to the cab driver, then inexplicably added: "I'm just a football hooligan."*

*Fenner arrived at Bedford with about fifteen minutes to spare before we went on stage. Our 'dressing room' was in the kitchen, and Fenner came in all flushed and sweaty, and started telling us about his train journey from Birmingham on what he called the Disoriented Express. Meanwhile, behind his back Andy was filling Fenner's uniform with cutlery from the kitchen drawers, tying the sleeves of his jacket into knots. He tied his shoelaces together too. We were now due to go on stage and once again Fenner was in a terrible state. "Goddammit," he muttered. "You bunch of ratbags."*

*As knives, forks and spoons clattered to the floor someone was heard singing, "Oh Mr Porter …".*

**John's Journal:**

### December 1973

*"Even during the war Christmases were better than this one's going to be," moaned Ron Bowden. We were travelling somewhere or other in the van and the subject of strikes and shortages had come up again.*

*"I wouldn't remember that far back," said Ted Baldwin slyly.*

*"No, you wouldn't, it was before the banjo was invented."*

*"Couldn't be. The banjo was invented on the 6th day. On the 7th God rested."*

*"He fucking well needed to. He probably would have wanted to commit suicide after that."*

*Points are awarded to winners of these arguments. It is a serious matter. Ron, who regularly totes two pints of bitter around like a pair of six guns, refers to Ted's banjo as the Frying Pan. To Ted, the sound of Ron Bowden's drums are Roadworks.*

### John's Journal: Sydney, Australia, 1977

*Ted Baldwin told us how he'd hailed a cab this morning, and directed it to the nearest health food shop. The driver had looked at Ted in amazement. "What you going there for?" he said.*

*"What for?" said Ted. "I need to buy some passion fruit juice, that's what for. I haven't had a crap for four days."*

*The cab driver was silent for a moment. "If you really want to give yourself the shits," he said thoughtfully, "why not buy yourself a cab."*

### Kenny:

When we were in Australia, near Brisbane, we stayed at Twin Towns. From there we travelled to gigs up and down the east coast. The thing they gave us to travel in was a minibus: a 'chicken coach'. In other words, it's owner sold chickens. And it had this enormous chicken on the roof. And there we were turning up at gigs with a giant chicken. People coming to our concerts must've wondered what they were going to get!

## John's Journal: Somewhere in Scotland, 1977

### 3 December

*... There was no stage at this club, and we were playing on the same level as the dancers who danced very close to the band. At one point a fellow with a metal hook instead of a hand gripped the end of my slide with this contraption and wouldn't let go. I stopped playing and told him to kindly remove himself (or words to that effect). Ken also lunged at him and said, "if you do that again I'll break your other arm," which sounded suitably threatening. But there was worse to come. A girl somehow got her long hair entangled with the water key on the end of my slide and couldn't get free. She sank to her knees and I was forced to sink to my knees too, and follow her around on all fours as she crawled across the room, trying to get free. I don't really know why, but I was still trying to play the tune amid the forest of knees belonging to the crowd of dancers while at the same time trying to calm this girl who was apparently in agony. Our pantomime must have looked very odd to a casual observer - as if we were taking part in some kind of strange fetish. We reached the far end of the hall where we freed ourselves; she in floods of tears and me soothing her like a child. All in all it was a very weird session.*

### Kenny:

On the night before the Royal Wedding of Charles and Diana in 1981 the band played at a ball in Buckingham Palace attended by royalty, heads of state and celebrities from around the world. There were about 1,500 of them - it was the biggest gathering of royalty in the whole of the twentieth century, I'm told. The band was set up in the Throne Room, and we played in front of the two thrones on a small stage about eight inches high.

I was bugling away and watching all those faces dancing by. After a while all I could see over the edge of my trumpet bell were bobbing tiaras.

171

We were invited to go to the marquee in the grounds afterwards for the disco and a bit of a knees-up. Afterwards I met Lady Diana, as she was then. A couple of weeks later we got a nice letter and a large piece of wedding cake.

### John:

*We started playing to an empty throne room. Of all people Spike Milligan was the first to appear. Then Lady Diana danced in with Prince Andrew. They were dancing very fast and as they went past the stage Diana slipped and nearly fell. I was in the middle of playing a solo on 'Getting Sentimental Over You' and as she regained her balance she caught my eye. She had these huge, dark blue eyes - and I completely lost it! It felt as if I'd received an electric shock! I just couldn't pick up the song again. Someone else took over and I was out of action for at least the next ten seconds!*

*Mind you, I'm easily distracted when playing trombone. Humphrey Lyttelton once said that if you see a jazz musician tootling away, eyes closed and looking dreamy, he's probably trying to remember whether he turned the gas off before he left home! With me, I get a touch of the mind-wanderings when I'm playing a tune I've played almost every night for the past umpteen years. Once, while playing 'Midnight in Moscow', I found myself composing a letter to the Wimpy hamburger company, praising them for the quality of their bean burgers - then suddenly found I'd crossed the beat. Crossing the beat is rather like entering a parallel universe. It's difficult, sometimes even impossible, to find your way back. The melody becomes foreign and the off beat becomes the on beat. Imagine marching on parade with an army unit, then turning left instead of right and unexpectedly finding yourself all alone and heading straight for the edge of a cliff.*

### Kenny:

We once played a charity gig in Abu Dhabi, attended by Prince Charles and Princess Diana. At the end of the gig, after we'd packed all the gear away and were waiting for a vehicle to pick it up, a black Mercedes reversed in. Then out of the venue came Prince Charles and Princess Diana. Instead of making straight for the car, Diana broke away and came over to chat to us. She spotted the huge bass case and said to John Benson, "Who have you got in there? Your mother-in-law?" I wonder what was on her mind!

All this time Charles had been left standing by the Mercedes, with the rear door open, glaring at her. Perhaps they'd had a tiff.

### John's Journal: Abu Dhabi, 1989

#### 15 March

*We are playing at the British Embassy. There was a sudden flicker of flash bulbs and people formed into a queue up to the verandah. Princess Diana, tall, in a beige dress, her face hidden behind the foliage, was shaking hands with the people passing along.*

*After our set we were taken up to the verandah. Roadie Pete Barnard did the honours, introducing Ken and the rest of us. Prince Charles said he had enjoyed our spot. "Are you going to play another one?" he asked.*

*"NO," replied Ken, perhaps a bit too emphatically.*

*"Oh …," said Prince Charles.*

*Ken then invited him down to our session in the hotel, as they are staying there too.*

*I can't remember anything of either of the Royal handshakes, except that Prince Charles took my attention away from Princess Diana by asking me, "How long have you been in the band?" Thirty years, I told him, and then I couldn't go back and shake Diana's hand again.*

*"It's this bloody jet lag," Prince Charles was saying to Ken later. "I get up in the morning, then I want to sleep again. How do you*

*manage with your lip. Do you get Lip Lag?"*

*I liked that; a genuine touch of the Spike Milligans. Charles seems very relaxed and has a good sense of humour. Diana is very tall; I think she is actually taller than me.*

### John's Journal: 4 December 1986

*Ken's old dad has died.*

### Kenny:

Dad went into a coma, and he must've been in that coma for five or six days in Chadwell Heath Hospital. My sister Marge and Doll, who was Dad's companion, were sitting by his bed holding his hand - he was spark out. And then suddenly he awoke and sat up! He asked for his oxygen mask to be taken off, so Doll, his 85-year-old 'live-in girlfriend', took it off. Then he said, "Give us a fuck, Doll." She quickly jammed the oxygen mask back on his face, and he went back into a coma and that was it. Those were his very last words. Absolutely true!

### John's Journal: 13 December 1986

*We're staying at Hatherley Manor near Gloucester. Last night Ken bought us all a drink on the memory of his Pop. Apparently Pop had left £25 in his will to buy the boys a drink after his death. We all drank to the Grand Old Man. He was only 18 months short of his congratulatory telegram from the Queen for his 100th birthday.*

*Ken told me some more of his family history. Ken's great-grandfather was born in the early 19th century, an illegitimate son of Lord Baldock. In his early years he worked in the kitchens of the lord's home. Later he became a bargee and sailed up to Bow, where he settled and worked as a builder. His son, Ken's grandfather, made stained-glass windows. Both lived into their 90s.*

*Ken's dad, whose first name was Jim, joined the Territorial Army as a boy soldier in 1902, just missing the Boer War but catching World War One in its entirety. His brother was gassed, and his brother's wife tried to earn money by picking fruit. While picking fruit she was struck by lightning and killed. Jim and his wife took their kids on. Then Jim's wife's sister went out to Australia to work on a banana plantation, got cancer and died. So Jim and his wife took on her kids too. Eventually there were 25 kids in the family, of which Ken is the youngest. His mum was 44 when she had him. What a sad, yet strangely uplifting story.*

### John's Journal: Tour of New Zealand with the Kenny Ball and Acker Bilk bands, 1989

*Acker, in the customs queue at Townsville, is in happy mood. He is singing to the tune of 'Stranger on the Shore': "There I stand, my scrotum in my hand, strangler on the floor ..."*
*"Mr Bilk," said the customs man, "are you any relation to Acker Bilk?"*
*"A very close relation," said Acker dryly.*

### 21 September
*Micky Cooke, trombonist with Acker, buys the 'curiously strong' mints, which are curiously horrible.*
*"Has anyone seen my mints?" he called.*
*"Walk up and down and let's have a look," said someone.*
*The prime minister of New Zealand is a trumpet player. Ken read out to us an item in the newspaper, a political dig comparing the prime minister to Nero; playing trumpet while Rome burned. There was silence for a moment while everyone digested this. "I thought Nero played tenor sax," chimed in Acker's trumpeter Mike Cotton.*
*Tony Pitt, who was once with Acker's band, was talking about their tour some years back of army bases in Malaya, and how the then*

175

*trumpeter Colin Smith, who'd never fired a gun in his life, was allowed to fire an Armalite on the range. Every third bullet was a tracer, and Colin was so surprised by the force of the recoil that his finger got stuck on the trigger. He was pushed back in the mud and the tracers went wildly away from the target and started whizzing over the border into Indonesia. A sergeant had to hurl himself across the gun barrel to prevent World War Three from starting.*

### John's Journal: Australia, The Kenny Ball and Acker Bilk bands cross the Nullarbor Plain, 1989

### 11 October

*The staff of the Australian domestic airlines are currently on strike and a note from our agent Paul Gadenne finally dispels any hopes of us flying to Perth. Seats in the coach have now been allocated. We'll be crossing the Nullarbor Plain non-stop, and it'll take us two nights and a day.*

### 12 October

*1 a.m. We are boarding our coach after the gig. Ron Bowden is offering everyone glasses of wine from his box. I nicked another pillow from the hotel, which made three in all. Everyone is nicking pillows; sorting out sleeping pills; getting settled.*

*"Fucking keeping us waiting!" growled Acker from his front seat. He is referring to his trumpeter Mike Cotton, who has yet to appear. There is a thing going on between Acker and Mike. Eventually Mike came on board and took the seat across the aisle from me. Acker followed him down: "Don't give me any shit," he said. "Don't argue or you might get one."*

*Vic the coach driver came down the aisle, stood between them and said, "Let's relax." There was no response from Acker, so Vic added a little more firmly, "Listen to me now! Sit down at the front."*

*Acker, ignoring Vic, said to Mike, "You're the worst argumentative bugger I've known. Don't rile me or I'll regret it for the rest of my life."*

*1.20 a.m. All is quiet again. But Mike Cotton is like John Fenner,
he just can't stop himself from arguing.*
*Down the front Acker, too, is still grumbling. "The longest haul
we've ever done or ever will do, and you go and piss off the coach."
(This, referring to Mike belatedly getting off to get himself a motel
pillow, having seen the rest of us with pillows.)*
*"I'd just like to inform everybody," said pianist Colin Wood,
helpfully, "that tomorrow is Friday the thirteenth."*

*2 a.m. After sitting silently for half an hour Mike went down the
front and the argument began again. I heard Mike in apologetic
vein say, "Let's let it go. I'm sorry. Let's leave it at that."*
*'Dutch' the second driver, not quite understanding, said, "You
fellows have been travelling under the worst conditions. Don't
apologise for being human."*

*4 a.m. All is now well. Ken took over the arbitration duties - and
everyone seems to have dropped off to sleep!*

*6.45 a.m. Blue skies, grassy plains, small bushes. Two pairs of blue
eyes appeared over the seat in front of me. "You 'wake?" "Wake up,
it's mawnin'." Two bright little voices; two bloody little nuisances.
Crystal and Melody; the harmonious names of the two kids that
belong to agent Paul Gadenne.*

*7.15 a.m. A kangaroo hopped across the road in front of us and off
across the plains.*

*8.30 a.m. Breakfast. I bought a 'We crossed the Nullarbor' postcard.
Although so far we haven't. We're still on the very edge of it; at a
place called Poochera. Sounds like a Spanish dog.*

*Midday. Nundroo. Glaring white sunlight but still plenty of wheat fields, grass, etc. And flies. "Flies are friendly," said the garage attendant. "They'll share your beer." He showed us an old telephone exchange, not now connected. "But still working perfectly," he said proudly.*

*As he touched it the dial fell out, and the receiver clattered onto the floor.*

*1.30 p.m. Stopped at the Nullabor service station.*

*2 p.m. The film High Society is playing on the coach video. "Who wants to be a millionaire?" "I DO!!" squawks everyone. In the film Louis Armstrong is playing 'Samantha' up-tempo: "We'll never get anywhere with that kind of music," Louis says., "What we need is a change of pace here," and then he plays the song as a ballad with Bing Crosby. The funny thing is, back in 1961 we did that in reverse - changed 'Samantha' from slow to up-tempo, and got into the hit parade with it.*

*2.30 p.m. The Great Australian Bight. We stopped for photos. Another coach had also stopped.*

*"It's rush hour here," someone remarked. It's always rush hour for flies. Huge swarms of them drove us back to our coach.*

*4 p.m. We crossed the border into Western Australia.*

*7.30 a.m. local time. Where did that night go? We have arrived at Perth.*

*I joined in the heartfelt round of applause for our drivers, and we all chipped in to give them a medal each, with an engraved plate. In return they said our two bands were great to get along with and we were all gentlemen. I wouldn't have gone as far as to say that.*

*"We crossed the Nullarbor," confided Ack to the audience at his*

*concert in Perth. There was a mighty cheer. Acker's band is going home tomorrow; we're off to Hong Kong. Mike Cotton has beaten his all-time best bird-spotting score: he recorded 200 birds. A new name has been suggested for our two bands: 'The Pork Hunts'. And that just about sums it up.*

### *Kenny:*

In 1983 the band was due to celebrate its 25th anniversary, and I had a great idea. Why not have a big get-together of the three most popular bands of the Trad Boom years - Chris Barber's, Acker Bilk's and mine? Great if we could stage it at the Festival Hall in London; better still if we could make a live recording of the proceedings.

That's just what we did. On 14 May 1983 the bands of Chris Barber, Acker Bilk and Kenny Ball - known as the Three B's - were brought together on stage for the first time in a generation for a concert at the Festival Hall. That concert has since been hailed as a milestone in the history of British jazz; an emotive experience for the bands as well as the audience. Many of the older fans, while still following the fortunes of the Three B's on record, TV or radio, hadn't been to a jazz club or a concert in years. A quarter of a century earlier they were the young ravers, the die-hard jazzers of the fifties and early sixties, who would've been present at every big jazz function: basking in the sunlight on riverboat shuffles, drinking themselves silly at open-air festivals, or propping open their eyelids in the smoky early hours of an all-night jazz jamboree. On this one night in the Festival Hall in 1983 it was just like old times.

When all 21 musicians of the Three B's got together backstage we had a right old laugh. Even though we work in different bands and travel separate ways most of the time, many of us are old drinking buddies, golf partners, or even one-time colleagues in the same band. From a musician's viewpoint, the professional traditional jazz world is almost like a family business.

And when, in 1985, the three bands went out on a nationwide tour together, it really felt as though we were one big band on the road.

### John's Journal: 1983

*In a loud voice John Benson is enquiring after complimentary tickets for the Three B's concert. He is told he can have two extra tickets.*

*"Good," he says grandly and deafeningly. "I want to bring my accountant and my solicitor."*

*"I don't blame you," growled Acker from his corner.*

*Ken likes the atmosphere of the three bands together. "It's like the old jazz jamborees," he says, "except there's a distinct absence of knee-trembling. Things ain't quite what they used to be."*

*To illustrate how things used to be, someone produced some old photos of the band. In the photos we were wearing large-collared shirts, tight jackets, flares, medallions, even beads.*

*"We were flower children back then," I said.*

*"What are we now?" muttered Ron Bowden. "Flour graders?"*

### Kenny:

The first and, as it turned out, only Three B's nationwide tour was over two weeks in September 1985. In the second tour, for six weeks in September/October 1986, Chris Barber's band was replaced by George Melly and John Chilton's Feetwarmers.

Five more tours followed, in 1988, 1990, 1991, 1993 and 1995, and the third acts in each case were respectively: Lonnie Donegan (as well as George Chisholm and Monty Sunshine); Kenny Baker (with Chisholm and Jack Parnell); Humphrey Lyttelton; Kenny Baker and Don Lusher (with Terry Lightfoot and Eric Delaney); and finally Humphrey Lyttelton and George Melly.

*On stage for the finale, Humphrey Lyttelton's trombonist Pete Strange and myself were wearing white jackets, while Micky Cooke, standing between Pete and I, was wearing his green satin waistcoat. Micky likened our appearance to a frog sandwich!*

*We launched into our big band trombone glissandos in 'Woodchopper's Ball', waving our slides up and down. "We sound just like Will Hay's fire engine," muttered Micky out the corner of his mouth. Mickey is the all-time world champ for making droll comments.*

### Kenny:

The Three B's still occasionally play together on single concerts, and of course my band often does double concerts with my old mate Acker. In 2009 the Three B's came together once more to play at the O2 Arena. It wasn't the very big O2 arena but the one they call 'Blue'. Maybe next time we'll go for the big one! The concert was a deal tied up with Universal: a very powerful company who'd bought the rights to all our old recordings. There were some people in the audience who actually believed it would be our very final concert together - how silly of them.

# 11
# MY GUYS

***Kenny:***

I've been very lucky with my musicians over the years. Of course, there have been one or two oddballs and fallings-out here and there. Not everyone is going to like you; that's impossible. There will always be the grumblers; it's the old thing about leaders taking more money than anyone else. But generally I've been lucky. A few of my players have been leaders themselves at one time, so they understand the problems. As far as I'm concerned, I try to run a friendly ship at all times; not like the old-time bandleaders who really were Hitlers. But, of course, in the end you've got to have one person who says, "That's the way it's going to be" - otherwise you've got a recipe for insanity, with everyone having a viewpoint and an equal say. I heard that was one of the reasons bandleader Alex Welsh actually took to drink. He ran what they call a 'co-operative' band - he didn't even take a leader's fee - and that helped to drive him to the vodka that eventually killed him.

So what about my good friends in the band? Well, perhaps closest of all is my trombonist John Bennett, who's been with me now in our band for nigh-on 53 years. John has been a terrific friend (and trombonist) for me, through thick and thin. He makes good suggestions for tunes ('The Green Leaves of Summer', which was a big hit for us, was his idea) and anytime we needed a new player in the band I always asked John what he thought. He's always been there for me and we've survived a few crises, too. I said this about John years ago when we were just starting the band, and it's still true: a particular thing about him is his humility. He's always willing to learn and I think that's why anybody who meets him takes an instant liking to him.

When we first started putting this book together John came to all the meetings, reminding me about dates and contributing some great memories too. John's very interested in people and, what's more, he's the band librarian: he's kept detailed scrapbooks all the way through our career. Plus he's a good photographer. And, of course, he was an outstanding player then, as he is now.

I remember when we started up John named his favourite trombone players as Lou McGarity and Abe Lincoln – which, of course, sets him apart from Chris Barber, or John Mortimer who was then with Acker Bilk's band. Chris liked everyone from Kid Ory to J.C. Higginbotham; the 'classic styles', I suppose you'd call them. And, of course, John Mortimer liked Trummy Young, who played with Louis for years in that kind of roaring style. Someone once called it 'demolition-squad trombone'. But John Bennett had this beautiful tone and a very fluid style, and I remember Steve Race saying in *Melody Maker*: "John plays with the fire of Trummy Young laced with flashes of Jack Teagarden's technical facility though his style is very much his own." Quite right - and a very nice compliment, too. Brian Matthews got it right as well, in my opinion, in his book *Trad Mad*, which came out in 1961 - a very handy guide to the trad scene, for which Brian told me he was paid £40 in all. In the book Brian said, "John is just about the finest trad trombonist in the country. His solo work is impeccable, his tone full and delightful at all times and his ensemble work the most tasteful imaginable." He also remembered that John has a gift for mimicry and used to do a very good impression of Elvis Presley on some of our wilder gigs. When John and I started out we had a very young band; it was a great band. We wanted a loose Dixieland outfit with a sort of Bobby Hackett/Jack Teagarden sound. We both had the same idea about that - and it proved to be a good one.

Anytime I wanted to do something, I always phoned up John. I'd say, "John, I want to do so-and-so, what do you think?" For instance, when we wanted a new piano player I had the choice of two and John said, well, forget the other bloke; we want Hugh Ledigo, because he's the more consistent player, less temperamental. And, as a result, we've had Hugh Ledigo now for what - 25 years! John and Hugh struck up a friendship - they play chess together. All that's beyond my comprehension. They're both tremendous chaps and I feel that, with myself and Andy, we are the stable people in the band. We are the roots, the core of the band, for want of a better way of putting it. Andy has been with us 45 years, Hugh 25 years and John 52 years. We've stuck together quite well. I'm very proud. And extremely happy.

But I should mention another side to John Bennett that our jazz fans may be unaware of: he is very … what can I call it? - accident prone. I remember on one occasion he entered a dressing room backstage, and on the wall there was a Red Cross cupboard. John walked up to it, and as he got near it the door opened and everything fell out. Lots of things like that have happened to John over the years.

### John:

*It's true. I do have some kind of paranormal influence on inanimate objects. Once I entered a pub just as our then roadie, Bill Bowyer, was about to throw a dart at the board. I looked at him, then at the board - and it fell off the wall! I was as surprised as everyone else, but people were very careful around me for a while after that.*

*I can trace it back to the early '70s when, during a BBC radio broadcast, I began a chain of events merely by glancing at a noticeboard on the wall. Without any help from me, several of the notices spontaneously detached themselves and fluttered to the carpet. I was so* astounded that I shot backwards and got my foot stuck in one of the large copper buckets that were used as ashtrays at the BBC. The next number was being counted in as I clattered up to the microphone like Long John Silver. When it ended, the only way I could get out of the bucket was to take off my shoe. At the time no one seemed to notice my Jacques Tati routine. But they soon became aware that there was something weird going on when a few minutes later I confessed to having accidentally locked my trombone in the dressing room. The broadcast was held up while security was called, keys were located and the instrument recovered. From then on our banjo/guitarist Ted Baldwin nicknamed me Lucky Jim.

My Lucky Jim episodes seem to have died down a bit in recent years. But there was a time when they seemed to up the stakes all by themselves. For a while I had a reputation as a walking disaster zone. When people saw me coming they'd step cautiously out of my path. Even now, Ken's always saying, "Don't let John touch that, it'll fall to bits."

One day I was seated alone in a Chinese restaurant and managed to drop a full bowl of rice upside down on the table. Don't ask me how I could've done that. Nothing too serious, I thought, while sheepishly scraping the rice back into the bowl with my knife. I shook my soy sauce bottle (as the directions stated) and watched helplessly as the lid came off and a gush of dark brown liquid rose into the air. For a moment it looked like the oil-strike scene from the film Giant. Then the spray settled, spattering the white tablecloth with countless brown freckles. The proprietor was standing nearby but luckily wasn't hit (as I was!) by flying soya. He regarded the ruined tablecloth, shook his head and smiled ruefully at me. So far, so fairly harmless. But there was far worse to come ….!

### Kenny:

John Bennett has actually had two people die during his trombone solos! The first time was in a big nightclub in Surrey. He'd just started playing 'Ory's Creole Trombone' when this guy leapt up from his table, started dancing, then just keeled over! They called two separate medic teams, who gave him a shot in his heart and carted him off. By that time we'd stopped playing, of course!

The next time was at a theatre in Bradford. John had only just launched into 'Ory's Creole Trombone' when we had to stop playing again - an old fellow had suffered a stroke. He was taken out into the corridor. In the interval John Bennett thought he'd go to the bar. He pushed the door to access the corridor and it banged up against something - turned out to be the head of the chap who'd just had a stroke!

### John:

*News got around fairly swiftly about my lethal trombone solo on 'Ory's Creole Trombone'. A trombonist friend of ours - Micky Cooke - who at that time had recently been sacked from the Terry Lightfoot band and was still smarting about it, even offered me £200 on condition I'd go and play that tune outside Terry Lightfoot's house!*

*I should mention, for those of a sensitive disposition, that I haven't played that number since!*

### Kenny:

Dave Jones, my clarinetist, on all the hit records of the 1960s bar one, was a tremendous musician. Actually, to begin with Dave wanted to be a trumpet player and started learning that. But then a friend of his had some records by the Benny Goodman Sextet and the very next day he went out and bought a simple-system clarinet (the one that has fewer keys but is actually harder to play) in Petticoat Lane. And from then on he was a big Benny Goodman fan. Before he joined us, Dave played with a lot of different bands: Len Beadle, Bobby Mickleborough's BobCats, Norman Cave - and Charlie Galbraith, where he first met me. But I think his best days were probably with us. Of course, he was on all the biggest hit records, and some of the tracks we did on the albums were marvellous. There's his 'High Society' on our second album, *Kenny Ball and his Jazzmen*, which some claim to be the best version ever put on record. That's the one where Dave and I play the famous clarinet chorus in harmony, which was very unusual back then.

Dave was quite a drinker - Carlsberg Specials for one thing - and when he was drunk he could be a very wild man indeed; he was known for that. It might've been partly because he was actually very nervous and often had to go into the dressing room and be sick before we did the show. But once he'd got drunk - oh dear. Once, on the Isle of Arran, we all had to double up in the rooms and Dave and I had to share a double bed. Now there was no question of any homosexuality between us - if you knew Dave and me at all, you'd know exactly how true that is. But I was the one who had to stay with him in the bed. So I kept my underpants and vest on and turned my back to face the wall, because I knew he'd be coming in pissed as usual. I remember one time when he arrived back - and I was desperately trying not to let him know that I was awake. Then I heard him open his clarinet case, take off his jacket and drop his trousers. And the next thing I heard I couldn't believe. So I opened one eye - and there was Dave, peeing into his clarinet case. He thought it was the toilet, because he'd had to lift the lid. I didn't know whether to laugh or cry, but I just kept quiet. And Dave didn't know anything about it until the next morning: "What's wrong with my fucking clarinet? And all the reeds are wet." And then, of course, I had to tell him. That was funny.

The end of our relationship came because of his drinking. It was awful really; I've done worse things myself and I've sometimes regretted it since. But this night we were playing in an American air base, somewhere near High Wycombe, and it was a real cabaret night. We had to be there on time and start on time, and there was a seated audience in front of us. And

American booze is strong. Anyway, they announced, "Ladies and gentlemen, Mr Kenny Ball and his Jazzmen" - and Dave wasn't there. He'd already had a few run-ins with me because of the booze, and I was fuming, as at this point we were really searching hard for work. The Beatles had arrived and the scene was changing. Then Dave suddenly appeared at the other end of the auditorium with two pints of beer in his hands and his clarinet under his arm, staggering, shoving through the audience and knocking into people. And, although I'm no kind of heavy disciplinarian, that was too much. I'd really had enough and told him, "That's it - you're out!" It was a Saturday night and we were due in Sunderland the following day. But that night I phoned Terry Lightfoot and he joined the band for a short time. It was my fault; I just couldn't take it. All I could think was, well, I've got to keep the band going somehow. But it seemed to affect poor Dave more than the rest of us.

Dave did deputise with us down in Torquay in 1981 for a couple of weeks, but he was very nervous again and got completely out of it. I think we were all drinking that night, but Dave managed to drink a whole bottle of vodka. Luckily, it didn't really matter, as there weren't a lot of people there that night. We were playing at the Palace Hotel, Torquay - a huge old hotel and very famous locally. It was once the Bishop's Palace. We played in the cabaret room downstairs, where the pianist Billy Munn used to work for years. The problem began when we played 'Them There Eyes', which is one of our most popular numbers. Clarinettist Andy Cooper, who joined us in 1967 after Terry Lightfoot left, usually sang one of the vocal parts in our routine, but this week he was away holidaying with his wife. Dave just didn't know what to do, so he started going around the room with his baritone, playing in people's ears and making a fool of himself really, and everybody knew he was pissed. He was trying to sing 'Them There Eyes' and it sounded horrible -

especially as he didn't know the arrangement. But at the same time it was very funny; we'll always remember it. And, even with his faults, Dave was our best deputy clarinettist.

After Dave left us he worked with several bands, including The Kinks' backing group - though I'm told they tried to make him look younger by giving him a long-haired wig! He did three years with Mike Cotton's band and even played in Carnegie Hall. Then later in the 1970s he worked with bands like Ron Russell's and spent nearly ten years with drummer Laurie Chescoe's band. Laurie ran a tiling company and gave Dave a job there, but the two of them spent more time on the road than in their day job.

Sadly, Dave died in 1999. I'll always remember him. He was a terrific player.

On banjo/guitar in the 1960s we had Paddy Lightfoot, Terry's younger brother. Paddy worked with us through all the greatest years, from 1961-70, and after he left us he went back to his brother Terry's band for a while. He gave up playing altogether more than 20 years ago, so far as I know.

Paddy had some wild moments, too. John Bennett was sharing a room with him one night, and Paddy got out of bed to go to the loo. However, being a bit disoriented he got in the wardrobe by mistake. John could see the furniture rocking about, silhouetted in the window, and then the whole thing fell down, bringing the window curtains with it. Somehow Paddy got out and went back to bed without a word. You know how in hotels back in those days they used to bring a tray of tea into the room in the morning? Well, on this occasion the lady got quite a surprise! But, leaving the tray on the dressing table, she too went off without a word!

Our band has had a few heavy drinkers in its time - like my first regular pianist, Ron Weatherburn (aka 'Weathers'), for instance. Ron was an absolutely marvellous solo player; his version of Jelly Roll Morton's 'Finger Buster' on our album *Kenny Ball and his Jazzmen* is really terrific. Ron joined us in summer 1960, replacing Barney Bates.

### John's Journal: Scotland, 1966

#### Tuesday 26 July

*We got to Forfar, where I shared a room with Ron Weatherburn. Weathers went out to buy some washing powder for his one and only shirt, and returning some time later blundered into the khazi where I was sitting composing my latest diary entry on a convenient roll of San Izal.*

*"I get my best ideas here," I explained sheepishly. Few of the band know that I am keeping a diary, and only Ron Weatherburn now knows that most of it has been written on loo paper. But nothing is too surreal for Ron Weatherburn. Muttering something about "fucking amateurs", Ron got his typewriter out of its case, lit a cigarette, donned his horn-rims and began tapping away at his latest novel like E.M. Forster. Feeling somewhat upstaged, I pocketed today's diary entry, pulled the chain noisily and mooched grumpily out for a cup of tea.*

*Later on, in the hotel bar, Ron Weatherburn came out with one of his famously loony pronouncements: "All well-known people," he intoned, "have rhythmic names."*

*"Like who?" I enquired.*

*"Like Aleister Crowley," replied Weathers. "If he had been common-or-garden 'Alastair' it would have messed up the rhythm and he would never have become famous." Furthermore, went on Weathers, Al-ei-ster Crow-ley, upon becoming famous, had suggested to the writer Dennis Wheatley that he follow his example by changing his Christian name to Dennison. Weatherburn paused while I digested that.*

*"So why didn't he?" I said at last.*

*"Because he's a cunt," replied Weathers, closing our philosophic
discourse with his usual subtlety.*

*Last night we played at Brighton Aquarium, the jazz club run by
Bonny Manzies, ex-hairdresser and wearer of a battered old straw
boater.*

*On the way home Weathers was sprawled out on the middle seat of
the band bus, fast asleep with his flies wide open. Dave Jones stuffed
a couple of ham and lettuce sandwiches in there. Then he painted
the whole area green with his felt-tip pen and stuck a clothes peg
where it would most hurt. It didn't even make Weathers' eyes water.*

### Kenny:

In the end, I couldn't put up with Ron Weatherburn anymore.
That was the trouble. Great musician though he was, as a soloist
you didn't know what you were going to get. He was an
epileptic, and during the ten years he was with the band he was
unknowingly taking the wrong medicine to control it. He'd
been prescribed phenobarbitone, and if you take that and then
drink alcohol you end up on the floor. And his favourite tipple
was brandy. Quite a few times he suffered epileptic attacks,
though never while on stage. But I remember we once stopped
at a transport café, and while queuing Ron collapsed. Someone
had to put a spoon in his mouth, as otherwise he could bite off
his tongue - and maybe swallow it, too. After he left the band he
did go very strange, and when you spoke to him it was as if he
were in another world. After he left us he did solo work and
played in trios, as well as Monty Sunshine, the local Eastside
Stompers from Ilford and Brian White's Magna Jazz Band. By
then he looked very different. You can see him in a Humphrey
Lyttelton TV documentary about the legendary trumpeter
Buddy Bolden, called *Calling My Chillun' Home*.

In 1995 Ron went to Toronto to appear with trumpeter Ken
Sims, whom he'd been playing with since the late 1980s, at their

Classic Jazz Society Festival, and he died in his sleep the night they got there. A very sad end to a great player.

After Ron, Johnny Parker joined me on piano. He'd been around for many years, playing with just about everyone from the late 1940s: Mick Mulligan, Humphrey Lyttelton for six years (Johnny Parker is the piano player on Humph's big hit 'Bad Penny Blues') and Alexis Korner's Blues Incorporated in the early 1960s. John depped for us during Ron Weatherburn's illness (I think it was 1967) and then worked for us full-time from 1970 to '78. And he could play anything: barrelhouse blues, delicate ragtime - whatever you needed, he could do it. A terrific player. And we used to love his dry sense of humour. He was married to the black South African singer-dancer Peggy Phango. One night we did a gig somewhere or another and we were looking down on the cabaret, which consisted of all these beautiful black women doing a limbo dance. And John said in bored tones, "I get all this stuff at home, you know."

John was great at dry one-liners. Once, when we were touring Switzerland, a couple of men came over to John and said, "Are you from Great Britain?"

John, in his posh Trevor Howard voice, said, "Yes, I am British actually."

To which these two cackled raucously, "It's not-so-Great Britain now, eh?"

John, unfazed, responded, "May I ask where you are from?"

"We are from Switzerland," they announced proudly.

"Ah," said John, "So you make cuckoo clocks."

"Nein! We do not make cuckoo clocks - they are made in Austria."

"Well, there you are then. You Swiss don't have much going for you if you can't even make a bloody cuckoo clock."

In the 1980s John got that nasty depressive disease called ME. He died in June 2010.

## John's Journal: Amsterdam, 1973

### 16 April
*John Parker was legless in more ways than one tonight after the gig. He kept colliding with things. To make matters worse, while he was in the pub someone pinched his walking sticks and went off with them. (Since his spinal operation John has needed two sticks to get around.) He was on his own at this point, and the only way he could haul himself back to our hotel was by vocally giving himself orders: "Come on now, Parker!" he bellowed. "Brace up! Remember you're British and among foreigners!"*

*Bill Bowyer heard the commotion from his second-floor bedroom window. He looked out just in time to see Parker vanish sideways through a hedge, from which he emerged on all fours. He made the last few yards to the hotel entrance in this quadruped fashion. Parker later told us how he had crawled past the receptionist on his hands and knees, and on to the stairway.        "Can I help you?" said the worried receptionist when he was halfway up the stairs on all fours. "No," said Parker, "... though on second thoughts, that's very kind of you, I'll have a gin and tonic please."*

## John's Journal: 1977

*"What would life be like without music?" said a starry-eyed but ageing female fan to John Parker.*

*"Peaceful," he replied.*

*"But how would you do your daily chores without music?" she persisted.*

*"You don't seem to understand, madam," answered John. "This **is** my daily chore."*

### Kenny:
John Parker's wife, Peggy Phango, was quite formidable - she'd

been known to threaten John with a knife, and also the great American cornettist Ruby Braff on one famous occasion. Peggy was a native South African from some Zulu tribe, but she'd escaped from the regime over there by coming to Britain with the musical *King Kong*, which was very big at the time. She had a great personality, as well as being built like a brick you-know-what, and the British pianist Keith Ingham irreverently used to call her 'Wagadugu', which is a historic township in Africa. But Peggy really did sing very well. One night she came to a party with John at my new house in Hornchurch, and I asked if she would mind playing a few tunes on my piano if I paid her, and she said, "No problem at all." Anyhow, she came along and got terribly pissed like everyone else. I don't think it took a great deal for her to get drunk anyway. Then she started arguing with Parker: "You bastard, Johnny bastard, I hate you, I'm going to kill you," etc. They were screaming and shouting at one another until eventually she said, "I'm going home," and just walked out of the door, miles from anywhere. John, stiff upper-lipped as always, said, "That just goes to show what can happen if you give the natives firewater."

What I remember most about Peggy were the arguments she would have with John in the back of the car when I was driving. She would actually beat him up in the back seat! Another time she hit him with a bedroom lamp while he was asleep and he turned up the next day with a terrible black eye. And once I was at home and got a phone call from John. She'd found out that Johnny was having an affair. They lived in a flat on the sixth floor in City Road, and John said, "Peggy's throwing a bit of a wobbly. She's hanging one of the children out of the window." So I got in my Roller and belted up to City Road at 100 miles an hour. By the time I got there she'd calmed down, but apparently she'd been threatening to kill the kids by throwing them out of the window. Of course, they're both grown up now, and in spite of all the tantrums that went on around them they were very normal, lovely kids.

Dealing with problems like drinking - well, although people might think differently, I'm very loyal. At least, I think I am. But unfortunately I've got this terrible cut-off point, which is awful. Once my mind is made up about someone, it's a kind of 'cut off my nose to spite my face' situation; that's it. My drummer for 40 years, Ron Bowden, was the most glaring example of that.

Ron was a bit older than the rest of us, and was two years my senior. Ron was a terrific drummer; he loved the music, played really well, and some of his early work was quite outstanding. Remember that great slow drum solo he plays on 'Tin Roof Blues' on our second album *Kenny Ball and his Jazzmen*? Ron was on all the hit records, but over the years he became very sour and disgruntled; he couldn't see the good side in anything. Then there were the usual accusations about me - "Oh, he's spending all our money" - and complaining about not getting enough. I think at one time in the 1960s we were earning about £180 a week. And that was a lot of money then. But he got more and more peeved and didn't even want to play certain tunes. So there am I - trying to sing, make the announcements, play the trumpet, pick the programme, keep everybody happy, smile at all the punters - and behind me there's someone who's disgruntled all the time. In the end, he wouldn't talk to anyone in the band. It just went on and on. I used to confide in my bass player, John Benson at that time, and say, "He's got to go. I can't take it."

Then something else started happening. Whenever I bent down to pick up one of my trumpet mutes - which were always left by the side of his drum kit, below the big cymbal - he'd crash that cymbal very loudly in my ear. He did it several times but always denied doing it on purpose. He knew what he was doing all right. He obviously hated me enough to give me an earache. And then one night we were playing 'The March of the Siamese Children' at the Mill Theatre at Sonning Eye near Reading. I bent down to pick up my straight mute as usual and he banged that cymbal so hard that I went completely deaf for about a minute. My hearing came back, luckily, but I was shaking my head and swore at him. There he was, looking innocent, but when we came off stage I said, "That's it." And that was it. He phoned the next day and asked, "Did you mean that?" and I said, "Yes, I did. I never want to see you again." And I meant it. It was the end. In a way, it was a similar story with John Benson. When the pair of them had gone I felt as though the shackles had at last been taken off me.

That sort of thing happens in bands. In Sid Phillips' band, George Bateman sat there for years and couldn't bear to look at Sid. I don't understand why people stay in bands like that. Okay, some bandleaders are notorious bastards - and sometimes they're called bastards whether they are or not. But I wouldn't want anyone to get the wrong idea. I've had a great life and I've met a lot of great people. And lots of them were in my band, too!

# 12
# TALKING ABOUT ME

*Kenny:*

Sid Phillips was a mentor to me. I didn't get along with him at first, but he was a terrific chap. If most of his musicians hated him, it was because he was so demanding as a musician. I learned to respect that. He didn't make me a great musician, but he made me think a lot about it. For instance, sometimes it's better to play fewer notes and leave gaps. That's quite essential in modern jazz, which sometimes sounds like millions of notes with no meaning. Sid's idea of jazz made sense: play the tune and let the people assimilate it.

Sid taught me arranging, and he told me what to do with the three-piece front line (in the nicest possible way, of course!) In fact, sometimes Sid taught me things without even knowing it. For instance, I learnt how to treat musicians with more respect than he did. He was one of the old school - he treated musicians as though they were his chattels. Over the five years that I was with him on and off, we'd arrive in a town for a gig and he used to drop us off outside his four- or five-star hotel. Then he'd walk in and that was it. The bus was locked up outside the hotel, you had a bag with you and you had your evening dress, and off you went to find a 15-bob bed and breakfast. Everybody made their own way to the gig afterwards.

When we formed our band, John and I, I said, "John, we're paying for the hotels, paying for bed and breakfast. And that comes out of the fee, because the guys are not going to go looking for bloody hotels after we arrive somewhere, because that's stupid. So we all stay together." And that's what we did, and what we always will do, even after 50 years. It's about treating musicians with respect. Okay, so we have to have a certain amount of discipline, otherwise we'd go bloody mad. You can't have seven people run a band as a committee.

I'm a bit of a student of people, I think. You've got to study people when you're a musician - you sense atmosphere. If you're a successful bandleader, you sense it even more because you can also sense the mood of an audience. And then, if necessary, you can change the programme - not so much with a concert perhaps, but certainly a dance. And one thing I've noticed in concerts: the audience don't like somebody who's over-confident; somebody who says, "Yes, well here I am …". It's much more acceptable just to say, "Well thank you for being here," and maybe be funny in your own way, naturally. People will enjoy that. But to try to make out you're full of confidence tends to look big-headed, and I've seen that in artists, in musicians, and it doesn't come across well to the audience. So I have a tendency to think: be yourself, smile, be nice and pleasant, tell a story if you want to, but don't say how wonderful you are. Instead, say how wonderful everybody else is. How much of that is *really* me, you might wonder. Honestly, all of it. I love the human race. Maybe some of them don't like me, but I've come to accept that. No one can be liked by everybody.

If heaven and hell do exist, you could live in heaven with a smile on your face if you're happy regardless of pressures. If you're permanently unhappy, well you're already living in hell in a way, aren't you? Of course, I've had challenges associated with being what I suppose you'd call a 'star' and also some playing problems over the years. I think it's probably perseverance that got me through - the persistence and determination that my dad had. How he survived four years in the First World War I'll never know, because he went straight into the trenches right at the beginning. He'd gone with the Territorial Army to Malta, and when the war started he sailed to Marseilles and travelled from there by truck right up to the front line, along with Indian troops, and then went through the whole war. I think to survive four years in the trenches you've got to be tough. Think about all the dirt, death, lice and everything. He was wounded twice, once in his shoulder and once in his head. He still had lumps of shrapnel wandering about in his head when he died. So from him I think I have the necessary iron streak.

But over the years I've had my own fears. I'd be a liar if I said I hadn't. Live television is one example; basically you shit yourself - mentally, that is, not physically, thank God! It's the fear of the unknown. However, if you prepare yourself and practise a lot that helps. I used to practise like mad - especially in the early years. After I left school - before I went into the army - I used to come home at lunchtime when I was working near to home and practise all through my lunch hour. I can remember doing that because I loved the trumpet, and the sound of music. Making music is such a joy, even now, 60-odd years later. I really, really enjoy it. I have my trumpet out of its case right now and I'll practise tonight.

My idea of jazz is to put a smile on people's faces - not make them want to shoot their brains out. But generally that sort of good time feeling seems to be happening less and less now, as the years go by. It seems that jazz is turning into some sort of underground music, when really it's out there to be played and enjoyed. When a musician or a band becomes commercially successful they're denigrated for it. But, of course, if you're paid, it's commercial. As long as you don't lose your own sense of integrity and you're talented enough to play your music well and put your heart and soul into what you do, then what's wrong with being 'commercial'? Louis Armstrong felt that way, didn't he? I love music. And I love seeing people smile. Back in 1973 I made a single with the Johnny Arthey Orchestra called 'Smile, Smile, Smile'. There were publicity stickers of a smiley face, with the logo 'Kenny Ball Says Smile'. We stuck them around everywhere, and I still come across them occasionally. (When we toured Russia our roadie even tried, unsuccessfully, to stick one on Lenin's tomb!) You've got to have fun. If you're lucky to have a 'sunny nature' it'll come out of the horn, won't it?

That's why I get a bit worried about modern music being so metallic and so electrical that it loses all its soul, for want of a better word. They talk a lot about soul these days – "crazy man, you got soul" - and, of course, there's what they still label 'soul music', although the sound of it has changed from what it was once. But it's not the type of music in itself that matters; it's the feeling in the music. You can sense it. I came to the conclusion maybe five or ten years ago that when any music becomes popular it's due equally to physical and mental effort. The listener watches your physical effort and at the same time, perhaps without even realising it, absorbs your personal emotions. If they like what they hear, they say, "That's wonderful." Maybe they don't know why they think it's wonderful, but actually it's because they've heard a musician's emotions broadcast to them directly. Honest emotions.

Maybe it's a bit like conversation. If you have a good conversation with somebody, there's a feeling of connection - and enjoyment - which is down to honesty. Then you might have a conversation where one person will dominate it, and that's different. A less honest conversation might happen if you're in illustrious or educated company. What you might do then is let the person talk about themselves, and you'll find they love that, and the result is that they think you're wonderful! It's just a trick, but it does work; I'm not knocking it. I learnt that from Charlie Chaplin, of all people. It was in his autobiography. When he first started meeting famous people and got lost for words, he used that trick. I've tried it - and it works.

When I first met Prince Charles I asked him, "How's it going on the ship?" because he was a naval captain then. And then, "How are you getting on, how are the girlfriends, and how's the trumpet playing?" I could talk to him about that because he did play the trumpet back then, so that's something we had in common. Originally, I think he started out on French horn, but he liked the trumpet better. When I first met him it was the first time he'd been to a nightclub, down near Guildford. I was sitting at the top table with Billy Butlin and his wife. Vera Lynn was on my right, and Eric Morecambe and Ernie Wise were sat further along, and so on - all the top names at the time were there. They put me opposite Prince Charles and I thought it was all very nice. Anyhow, I managed to find out which knife and fork to pick up and, of course, Charles was very nice, saying, "I've got some of your records, Ken," and it was all going well. But then towards the end of the meal a bloke came up and said, "You'd better come and get ready now, Ken." So I got up from my chair and went backstage to get my trumpet and get ready to blow. And then I realised that they'd asked me to move so that Prince Charles could get a clear view of the stage.

I've done a lot of composing over the years. Some years ago I wrote the theme song for a film directed by Richard Attenborough. I think it was called *The Blockhouse*. It starred Peter Sellers, and in the movie he was supposed to be in prison. Dickie said, "Come on the set to get the atmosphere," so I could write the song. Well, Peter was already in this cell when I got on set, and as I walked past him he just nodded, as he was getting into character and really was in world of his own, so we didn't have a conversation. But Dickie's really a very nice chap. So anyhow, I wrote the tune for him (in fact, I think I offered him about three in all) and they sent me a cheque for £500. But they never used the tune - in fact, they never used any music for the film at all. So I suppose I could've called it 'The Money Song' or the 'Filthy Lucre Tune' or something like that. I've seen Dickie Attenborough a couple of times since, but that's the only time we worked together.

I've written many tunes in my time, and over the last year I've been writing a hell of a lot. I wrote a really nice one for a band the other day and since then I've written at least four more. I'll write 20 songs and one will be good. There was one I liked a lot called 'Fleet Street Lightning'. At that time - probably 1960-61 - I was working with the band every week, resident on a lunchtime session at the famous Fleet Street Jazz Club, which was run by the tenor saxist Ray Whittam. Much later, John Benson, my bass player for a while, put me off writing tunes, picking on 'Fleet Street Lightning' as corny and sounding like something else. The funny thing is, my clarinet player, Andy Cooper, plays 'Fleet Street Lightning' with his own band, The Euro Top Eight. And he's recorded it, too.

I never talk down to people, you know - I'm not like that. Not at all. But I do remember just once coming back from a late gig on the A1 to pick up some diesel at a service station. I joke about it now actually. We all piled out of the wagon and this attendant - bloody arrogant he was - had just washed his floor.

He said, "You can't come in here. You can't come in here!"

So I said jokingly, "Don't you know who I am?"

And he replied, "Who are you then?"

So I said, "Kenny Ball."

To which he replied, "I don't care if you're Kenny Dalglish - just fuck off."

# EPILOGUE

Phew! It's about time I had a break. Have we got enough for a book yet?

*We've got enough for one book - and there's still plenty more where that came from.*

Perhaps we ought to call it Volume One, then.

*Good idea. I'll start taking notes now.*

Right, see you on the battlefront. Ta-ta, mate.

*Cheers, Ken. Here's to the next gig - and the next 50 years!*

www.apexpublishing.co.uk